HEALTH CARE REFORM ACT: CRITICAL TAX AND INSURANCE RAMIFICATIONS

BY JANEMARIE MULVEY, PH.D.

Notice to Readers

Health Care Reform Act: Critical Tax and Insurance Ramifications is intended solely for use in continuing professional education and not as a reference. It does not represent an official position of the Association of International Certified Professional Accountants, and it is distributed with the understanding that the author and publisher are not rendering legal, accounting, or other professional services in the publication. This course is intended to be an overview of the topics discussed within, and the author has made every attempt to verify the completeness and accuracy of the information herein. However, neither the author nor publisher can guarantee the applicability of the information found herein. If legal advice or other expert assistance is required, the services of a competent professional should be sought.

You can qualify to earn free CPE through our pilot testing program.
If interested, please visit aicpa.org at http://apps.aicpa.org/secure/CPESurvey.aspx.

Course Code: **745817**
CL4HCRA GS-0417-0A
Revised: **March 2017**

TABLE OF CONTENTS

Recent Developments

Users of this course material are encouraged to visit the AICPA website at www.aicpa.org/CPESupplements to access supplemental learning material reflecting recent developments that may be applicable to this course. The AICPA anticipates that supplemental materials will be made available on a quarterly basis. Also available on this site are links to the various "Standards Trackers" on the AICPA's Financial Reporting Center which include recent standard-setting activity in the areas of accounting and financial reporting, audit and attest, and compilation, review and preparation.

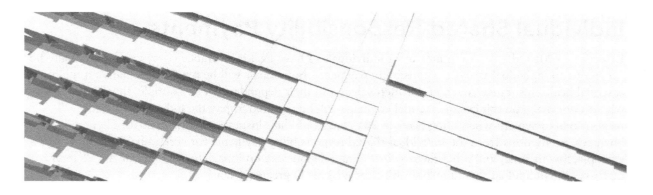

Chapter 1

INDIVIDUAL SHARED RESPONSIBILITY PAYMENTS AND PREMIUM TAX CREDITS FOR INDIVIDUALS

LEARNING OBJECTIVES

After completing this chapter, you should be able to do the following:

- Identify what insurance qualifies as minimum essential coverage.
- Identify exemptions from individual shared responsibility payments when individuals do not have minimum essential coverage.
- Estimate the individual shared responsibility penalty under different assumptions about income and family size.
- Identify factors affecting eligibility for premium tax credits under the Patient Protection and Affordable Care Act (ACA).
- Estimate premium tax credit under different income levels.
- Calculate amount of premium tax credits that must be reconciled to income tax returns.

Individual Shared-Responsibility Payments

Effective in 2014, the ACA requires most individuals to have health insurance coverage or potentially be subject to an individual shared responsibility payment.[1] Individuals will be required to maintain minimum essential health insurance coverage for themselves and their dependents. For example, those individuals who do not maintain minimum essential coverage will be required to pay the individual shared responsibility payment when filing taxes in 2017 based on their insurance status in 2016. There are, however, exemptions from the individual shared responsibility payments for certain hardships (for example, low income) and other factors, including religious exemptions. The first half of this chapter discusses the individual shared responsibility provisions in greater detail.

The second part of this chapter explores the ACA premium tax credits, which are intended to improve affordability for the purchase of health insurance coverage for low and middle-income taxpayers.

MINIMUM ESSENTIAL COVERAGE

Individuals are required to have minimum essential coverage. The following types of coverage qualify as minimum essential coverage:

- Coverage under a government sponsored plan, including the following:
  - Medicare Part A
  - Medicare Advantage Plans
  - Most Medicaid coverage[2]
  - The State Children's Health Insurance Program (CHIP)
  - Most types of TRICARE
  - Comprehensive health programs offered by The Department of Veterans Affairs
  - Department of Defense Nonappropriated Fund Health Benefits Program
  - Coverage provided to Peace Corps volunteers
  - Refugee Medical Assistance
  - Coverage through a Basic Health Program (BHP) standard plan
- Employer-sponsored coverage, with respect to any employee, including the following:[3]
  - Self-insured plans, COBRA coverage, and retiree coverage
  - Coverage under an expatriate plan for employees and related individuals
  - Group health insurance coverage for employees under
    - a plan or coverage offered in the small or large group market within a state,
    - a plan provided by a governmental employer, such as the Federal Employees Health Benefit Program, or
    - grandfathered health plans offered in the group market[4]

---

[1] ACA Section 1501(b) enacted IRC Section 5000A.

[2] Medicaid programs that provide limited benefits generally don't qualify as minimum essential coverage. However, individuals with certain types of limited-benefit Medicaid coverage qualify for a coverage exemption. See Table 1.1 in this chapter.

[3] This coverage requirement is different than other requirements relating to potential employer penalties such as adequacy and affordability or type of benefits required.

[4] A grandfathered health plan refers to an existing plan in which at least one individual has been enrolled since enactment of the ACA (March 23, 2010). To maintain grandfathered status, a plan must avoid certain changes to employer contributions, access to coverage, benefits, and cost-sharing.

- Individual health coverage
  - Health insurance you purchase directly from an insurance company
  - Health insurance you purchase through the marketplace
  - Health insurance provided through a student health plan
  - Catastrophic coverage
  - Coverage under an expatriate health plan for non-employees such as students and missionaries
- Other Coverage
  - Certain foreign coverage
  - Certain coverage for business owners
  - Coverage recognized by the U.S. Department of Health and Human Services (HHS) as minimum essential coverage

Minimum essential coverage does not include health insurance coverage consisting of excepted benefits, such as dental-only coverage. However, the IRS does specify that the existence of limited Medicaid coverage exempts individuals from the individual mandate for months in 2015 in which individuals were covered under certain limited-benefit government-sponsored programs. The specific programs that fall within this category are Medicaid programs that provide the following:

- Optional family planning
- Optional coverage of tuberculosis-related services
- Coverage of pregnancy-related services
- Coverage limited to treatment of emergency medical conditions
- Coverage for medically needy individuals
- Coverage under waivers programs

EXEMPTIONS

Uninsured individuals who meet certain criteria are exempt from the individual shared-responsibility provision and will not have to obtain coverage or make shared-responsibility payments when they file their tax return.

Depending on the type of exemption, it is obtained either through the exchange or through the IRS. All exemptions are to be reported on an individual's tax return, except those automatically exempt from filing a tax return because their income is less than the tax filing threshold (see table 1-1).

Although the exemptions listed in table 1-1 are generally straightforward, a more complicated exemption exists for citizens living abroad and certain noncitizens. This includes exemptions for the following circumstances:

- A U.S. citizen or a resident alien who was physically present in a foreign country or countries for at least 330 full days during any period of 12 consecutive months
- A U.S. citizen who was a bona fide resident of a foreign country or countries for an uninterrupted period of time that includes the entire tax year
- A bona fide resident of a U.S. territory
- A resident alien who was a citizen or national of a foreign country with which the United States has an income tax treaty with a nondiscrimination clause and who was a bona fide resident of a foreign country for an interrupted period that includes the entire tax year

- Not lawfully present in the United States and not a U.S. citizen or U.S. national (For more information of who is treated as lawfully present in the United States for purposes of this coverage exemption see www.healthcare.gov.)
- A nonresident alien, including (1) a dual-status alien in the first year of U.S. residency or (2) a nonresident alien or dual status alien who elects to file a joint return with a U.S. spouse (This exemption does not apply if you are a nonresident alien for 2016, but met certain presence requirements and elected to be treated as a resident alien.[5])

CLAIMING AN EXEMPTION ON TAX RETURNS

Tax filers can claim or report coverage exemptions on Form 8965, *Health Coverage Exemptions*, and file it with their Form 1040, Form 1040A, or Form 1040EZ. However, if a household's gross income is less than the applicable minimum threshold for filing a federal income tax return, they are exempt from the individual shared responsibility provision and are not required to file a federal income tax return solely to claim the coverage exemption. If you file a return anyway (for example, to claim a refund), you can claim your coverage exemption with your return.

Exemptions granted from the exchange (marketplace) will be sent with a unique exemption certificate number (ECN). Tax preparers will enter the ECN in Part I, *Marketplace-Granted Coverage Exemptions for Individuals*, of Form 8965 in column C.

If the marketplace has not processed an exemption application before a tax return is filed, tax preparers should complete Part I of Form 8965 and enter "pending" in Column C for each person listed. In this case, the tax filer does not need the ECN from the marketplace.

For coverage exemptions issued by the IRS directly, a tax preparer needs only to file Form 8965, there is no need to call the IRS in advance to obtain the exemption.

Part II of Form 8965 entitled: *Coverage Exemptions for Your Household Claimed on Your Return*, is used to claim a coverage exemption if a filer's income is less than the filing threshold and he or she still wishes to file a tax return. However, filing a tax return for this particular exemption is not necessary and only optional.

Other coverage exemptions may be claimed on tax return using Part III, *Coverage Exemptions for Individuals Claimed on Your Return*, of Form 8965. Use a separate line for each individual and exemption type claimed on the return.

---

[5] For more information see IRS Pub. 519.

Table 1-1 Individual Mandate Exemptions

Exemption	Available Through	Code for Exemptions
Members of certain religious sects	Exchanges	Need ECN
Short coverage gap (<3 consecutive months)	IRS	B
Citizens living abroad and certain noncitizens	IRS	C
Coverage is considered unaffordable (exceeds more than 8.13% of household income)	IRS	A
Coverage is considered unaffordable based on projected household Income	Exchange	Need ECN
Aggregate self-only coverage considered unaffordable (exceed 8.13% of household income)	IRS	G
Household income less than the tax filing threshold	IRS	No code necessary see Part II Form 8965
Member of tax household born or adopted during the year	IRS	H
Member of tax household died during the year	IRS	H
Members of federally recognized Indian tribes	Exchanges or IRS	E
Members of health care sharing ministries	Exchanges or IRS	D
Incarceration	Exchanges or IRS	F
Resident of a state that did not expand Medicaid	Exchanges	G
Certain Medicaid programs not considered minimum essential coverage	Exchanges	Need ECN
Unable to renew existing coverage	Exchanges	Need ECN
Certain Medicaid programs that are not considered minimum essential coverage (for example, benefits targeted toward pregnant woman or spend-down programs)	Exchanges	Need ECN
General hardships and unable to obtain coverage under a qualified health plan	Exchanges	Need ECN

Source: IRS Form 8965 Instructions 2016, https://www.irs.gov/pub/irs-pdf/i8965.pdf

FORMULA FOR DETERMINING INDIVIDUAL SHARED RESPONSIBILITY PAYMENTS

Individuals who do not receive an exemption and do not have minimum essential coverage may be required to pay a penalty for each month they do not have coverage. The amount of the penalty is the greater of a fixed dollar amount or a percentage of income, but applies only to household income greater than the federal tax filing requirement thresholds.

Household income is based on modified adjusted gross income (MAGI), which equals adjusted gross income from an individual's tax return plus any excludable foreign earned income and tax-exempt interest income received during the taxable year. Household income also includes the income of all dependents who are required to file tax returns. Unlike the premium tax credit MAGI definition, the MAGI calculation used for the individual shared responsibility payment formula does not include non-taxable Social Security benefits.

For 2016, the annual individual shared responsibility payment amount is the greater of

- 2.5 percent of household income (MAGI) that is greater than the tax return filing threshold based on an individual's tax filing status (see table 1-3), or
- a flat dollar amount based on family size, which is $695 per adult age 18 and older, and $347.50 per dependent younger than age 18, limited to a family maximum of $2,085.

Potential individual penalties are capped at the cost of the national average premium for a bronze-level health plan available through the exchanges. In 2016, individual penalties are capped at $2,676 per individual ($223 per month) and $13,830 for a family of five or more members ($1,115 per month).[6]

KNOWLEDGE CHECK

1. A married couple has no health insurance coverage in 2016. Their total MAGI in 2016 was $27,000. Assume they are not eligible for any exemptions. How much will they pay in the individual shared responsibility payments for tax year 2016?

    a. $675.
    b. $1,390.
    c. $157.50.
    d. $650.

Though initial individual penalties are relatively small in the initial year of implementation, they increase significantly in later years and are adjusted for inflation in the longer run. As shown in table 1-2 the share of income rises from 1 percent in 2014 up to as high as 2.5 percent of MAGI adjusted for tax filing thresholds in 2016 and beyond.

---

[6] IRC Rev. Proc 2015-15.

Table 1-2 Amount of Individual Penalty

		Greater of
2014	1% × (Household Income – Tax Filing Threshold)*	$95 per household member older than age 18 + $47.5 per dependent younger than age 18 *Capped at $285 per household*
2015	2% × (Household Income – Tax Filing Threshold)*	$325 per household member older than age 18 + $162.50 per dependent younger than age 18 *Capped at $975 per household*
2016	2.5% × (Household Income – Tax Filing Threshold)*	$695 per household member older than age 18 + $347.50 per dependent younger than age 18 *Capped at $2,085 per household*
2017 and Beyond	2.5% × (Household Income – Tax Filing Threshold)*	$695 (times inflation adjustment) per household member older than age 18 + $347.50 (times inflation adjustment) per dependent younger than age 18 *Capped at 300% of flat dollar amount*

Note: Household income is modified adjusted gross income.

*The total penalty cannot exceed the national average premium for bronze-level plans offered through the exchanges (for the relevant family size). In 2016, this is equal to $2,676 per individual ($223 per month) and $13,380 for a family of five or more members ($1,115 per month).

Proof of Health Insurance Coverage

In tax year 2017 and subsequent years, individuals will have to submit proof of coverage when they file their taxes each year. Both insurers and employers are to report to the IRS and submit statements to individuals showing that they are providing minimum essential coverage on IRS Forms 1095-B and 1095-C to workers and covered individuals. Individuals who receive coverage through the health insurance exchange will receive a Form 1095-A from the exchange.

However, because of continual delays in filing date, the IRS provided additional guidance in late December of 2016 for tax year 2016 individual tax return filings. Because the employer due dates for filing forms 1095-B and 1095-C to individuals were extended to March 2, 2017, individuals will not be required to furnish a copy of form 1095-B to the IRS to document their health insurance coverage but must keep copies for their files.

Table 1-3 2016 Federal Tax Filing Thresholds For "Most" People

Filing Status	Age	Gross Income** Must Exceed
Single	Under 65	$10,350
	65 and Older	$11,900
Head of Household	Under 65	$13,350
	65 and older	$14,900
Married Filing Jointly	Under 65 (both spouses)	$20,700
	65 and older (one spouse)	$21,950
	65 and older (both spouses)	$23,200
Married Filing Separately	Any age	$4,050
Qualifying Widow with Dependent Children	Under 65	$16,650
	65 and older	$17,900

Source: IRS, Form 8965 Instructions 2016, https://www.irs.gov/pub/irs-pdf/i8965.pdf

Table Notes: If you were born on January 1, 1952, you are considered to be age 65 at the end of 2016. (If your spouse died in 2016 or if you are preparing a return for someone who died in 2016, see IRS Pub. 501).

**Gross income means all income you received in the form of money, goods, property, and services that isn't exempt from tax, including any income from sources outside the United States. It also includes gains from the sale of your main home even if you can exclude part or all of it. Include only the taxable part of social security benefits (Form 1040, line 20b, Form 1040A, line 14b). Also include gains, but not losses, reported on Form 8949 or Schedule D. Gross income from a business means, for example, the amount on Schedule C, line 7, or Schedule F, line 9. But in figuring gross income, don't reduce your income by any losses, including any loss on Schedule C, line 7, or Schedule F, line 9.

KNOWLEDGE CHECK

2. In which tax year will individual tax filers first be required to provide 1095-B documentation to the IRS to prove they have health insurance coverage?

    a. 2014.
    b. 2015.
    c. 2016.
    d. 2017.

FAILURE TO PAY INDIVIDUAL SHARED RESPONSIBILITY PAYMENTS

Taxpayers who are required to pay a penalty but fail to do so will receive a notice from the IRS stating that they owe the penalty. If they still do not pay the penalty, the IRS can attempt to collect the funds by reducing the amount of their tax refund in future years. However, individuals who fail to pay the penalty will not be subject to any criminal prosecution or other financial penalty for such failure. The secretary of HHS cannot file notice of lien or file a levy on any property for a taxpayer who does not pay the penalty.

KNOWLEDGE CHECK

3. What is the fine for not paying an individual shared responsibility payment that is owed to the federal government?

    a. 25 percent of amount owed + monthly interest.
    b. Imprisonment.
    c. Lien on property.
    d. No additional fine levied.

MAGI

Determining a tax filing unit's MAGI is an integral part of the following ACA provisions:

- Individual shared responsibility payments
- Eligibility for premium tax credits
- Employer-shared responsibility payments affordability criteria
- Expansion of Medicaid
- Income thresholds for high-income taxes (in other words, additional Medicare tax and net investment income tax)

Yet, income included in or excluded from MAGI across these provisions is not consistent. The main difference is whether non-taxable Social Security benefits are added back to MAGI. When the law was originally written and enacted, MAGI for purposes of premium tax credits did not include non-taxable Social Security benefits. Therefore, early retirees receiving Social Security benefits could more easily qualify for premium tax credits and Medicaid if a portion of their Social Security benefits were not taxed. This was changed subsequently under P.L. 112-56. However, it only affected three of the five ACA provisions relying on MAGI (see table 1-4); it did not affect the others. Non-taxable Social Security benefits are also included in MAGI for determining whether an employer plan is affordable and for determining Medicaid eligibility.

Table 1-4 Definition of MAGI Across ACA Provisions

ACA Provisions	Included in MAGI			
	Adjusted Gross Income	+ Tax-Exempt Interest	+ Foreign Earned Income	+ Non-Taxable Social Security Benefits
Individual Shared Responsibility Formula	Yes	Yes	Yes	No
Premium Tax Credits	Yes	Yes	Yes	Yes
Affordability Criteria for Employer Penalty	Yes	Yes	Yes	Yes
Medicaid Expansion	Yes	Yes	Yes	Yes
Net Investment Income Tax Threshold	Yes	Yes	Yes	No

KNOWLEDGE CHECK

4. Which ACA provision does NOT include non-taxable Social Security benefits in MAGI?

    a. Affordability criteria for employer penalty.
    b. Net investment income tax threshold.
    c. Premium tax credits.
    d. Medicaid expansion.

Premium Tax Credits for Individuals

The ACA provides premium tax credits to individuals (including the self-employed) if their household income is less than certain thresholds, and if they purchase coverage through the individual health insurance exchanges.[7] The lower a household's income level, the larger the value of the credit. Though the maximum income threshold for 2016 enrollment is $47,080 for single filers and $63,720 for married filers residing in the 48 contiguous states, individuals at the higher income thresholds may receive a very small credit. The tax credit is refundable in that an individual can still receive a credit that is greater than his or her taxes owed.

The self-employed face an advantage in qualifying for premium credits because income for eligibility purposes excludes business expenses as well as other self-employed deductions from income, such as contributions to qualified retirement plans.

The following section details the eligibility requirements for the premium credit and the formula for determining the amount of the premium credit and the timing of the credit. Though this information is presented in the context of the self-employed, the premium tax credit is available to any individual who meets the eligibility criteria, regardless of employment status.

ELIGIBILITY FOR PREMIUM TAX CREDITS

An individual must meet the following criteria to be eligible for premium tax credits:

- Have household income less than specific thresholds
- Purchase health insurance through the state's individual exchange[8]
- Be ineligible for other sources of health insurance coverage
- Cannot file *married filing separately* (unless special circumstances, including victim of spousal abandonment or of domestic violence).

Household Income Thresholds for Eligibility

Individuals must have MAGI within certain thresholds to be eligible for premium tax credits. The MAGI is defined as adjusted gross income plus tax-exempt income and foreign income. The MAGI for purposes of eligibility for premium tax credits also includes the nontaxable portion of Social Security benefits.

There are some tax advantages for the self-employed and other pass-through entities, as income under this definition allows exclusions for certain self-employed expenses such as contributions to qualified retirement plans like Simplified Employee Pensions and SIMPLE plans. Those close to the income limits face an incentive to increase retirement contributions to gain a larger premium tax credit.

The MAGI thresholds for eligibility of premium credits are compared to the federal poverty guidelines (also called federal poverty level). To be eligible for premium credits, an individual's MAGI must be at or greater than 100 percent of the federal poverty level (FPL), but no more than 400 percent of the FPL.

---

[7] The ACA, Section 1401(a), enacted IRC Section 36B.

[8] States have the option to either: (1) set up their own state-based exchange, (2) rely on the federal government exchange, or (3) develop a partnership with the federal government.

The federal poverty guidelines published by HHS for the year prior to enrollment are used to determine income eligibility. For example, the 2015 federal poverty guidelines are used to determine the income threshold for the 2016 open enrollment period that began November of the prior year.

Table 1-5 Minimum Income for Premium Credit Eligibility in 2016 (100 Percent of Federal Poverty Level)

Number of Persons in Family	Modified Adjusted Gross Income		
	48 Contiguous States and DC	Alaska	Hawaii
1	$11,770	$14,720	$13,550
2	$15,930	$19,920	$18,330
3	$20,090	$25,120	$23,110
4	$24,250	$30,320	$27,890
5	$28,410	$35,520	$32,670
6	$32,570	$40,720	$37,450
7	$36,730	$45,920	$42,230
8	$40,890	$51,120	$4,010

Note: Eligibility for 2016 premium tax credits are based on 2015 Federal Poverty Levels.

The FPL varies by family size and whether a household lives in the contiguous states, Alaska, or Hawaii. The minimum income level base is 100 percent of the federal poverty level (see table 1-5). It is important to note that premium credits are not available to individuals who have less than 100 percent of the federal poverty level. The intent was that these individuals would enroll in the new expanded Medicaid program (available up to 138 percent of FPL). But, the Supreme Court ruled that the federal government could not force states to expand Medicaid. Therefore, there is a coverage gap in those states that did not expand Medicaid for individuals with income less than 100 percent of FPL. The one exception to this is that lawfully present immigrants whose household income is less than 100 percent FPL and are not otherwise eligible for Medicaid are eligible for tax subsidies through the marketplace if they meet all other eligibility requirements.

The maximum income level for an individual to qualify for premium credits in 2016 is 400 percent of the FPL, adjusted for the number of persons in the family (table 1-6). This equals $47,080 if single, $63,720 married, or $80,360 with one child and $97,000 with two children residing in one of the 48 contiguous states or DC.

Table 1-6 Maximum Income for Premium Credit Eligibility in 2016 (400 Percent of Federal Poverty Level)

	Modified Adjusted Gross Income		
Number of Persons in Family	48 Contiguous States and DC	Alaska	Hawaii
1	$ 47,080	$ 58,880	$ 54,200
2	$ 63,720	$ 79,680	$ 73,320
3	$ 80,360	$100,480	$ 92,440
4	$ 97,000	$121,280	$111,560
5	$113,640	$142,080	$130,680
6	$130,280	$162,880	$149,800
7	$146,920	$183,680	$168,920
8	$163,560	$204,480	$188,040

Source: Based on HHS 2015 Poverty Guidelines, available at: http://aspe.hhs.gov/poverty/15poverty.cfm.

KNOWLEDGE CHECK

5. Which income level disqualifies a family of three living in Hawaii for a premium tax credit in 2016?

    a. $54,200.
    b. $95,000.
    c. $80,500.
    d. $73,500.

Purchase Coverage Through an Individual Exchange

Premium tax credits are available to individuals (including the self-employed) only if the health insurance coverage is purchased through the individual exchanges.[9] To be eligible to enroll in an individual exchange, the taxpayer must

1. reside in a state in which an exchange is established;
2. not be incarcerated, except individuals in custody pending the disposition of charges; and[10]
3. be a "lawfully present" resident.[11]

There are generally limits on the time period in which individuals can enroll in the health insurance exchanges. The open enrollment period for the exchanges generally occurs from November until January of the following year. There are, however, exceptions outside of the open enrollment period due to changes in life events such as divorce, loss of job, or the birth of a child. So, if a person becomes self-employed after losing a job, he or she may be able to apply with a special enrollment period. If the person voluntarily left his or her job and lost coverage, he or she does not qualify for the special enrollment period and would have to enroll during the specified open enrollment period.[12]

Eligibility for Other Health Insurance Coverage

In order to be eligible for a premium tax credit, individuals cannot be eligible for other health insurance coverage through public or private sources. This other coverage is referred to as *minimum essential coverage*. The following types of insurance coverage qualify as minimum essential coverage, and if a self-employed individual is eligible for any of these, he or she would not be eligible for premium tax credits:

- Medicare (Part A, Advantage)
- Medicaid
- Tricare
- Tricare for Life (a VA program)
- Federal Employee Health Benefits Program
- An employer-sponsored plan that is *adequate* (60 percent actuarial value) and *affordable* (does not exceed 9.5 percent (as adjusted for inflation) of household income)
- Coverage on the SHOP exchange[13]

Exceptions to Minimum Essential Coverage. The ACA does provide some exceptions to minimum essential coverage whereby individuals who have the following coverage can still be eligible for premium credits if they meet the other criteria:

- An individual who is only eligible to obtain coverage through the individual (non-group) health insurance market
- An individual who is eligible for an employer-sponsored plan that is *not deemed* adequate or affordable
- An individual who is eligible for limited benefits under Medicaid

---

[9] Exchanges in this case are the publicly available exchanges and should not be confused with private exchanges offered by employers and other private entities.

[10] Final regulations state that family members of incarcerated individuals may enroll in the exchange and receive premium credits as long as they meet the other eligibility criteria (see 77 FR 30377, May 23, 2012).

[11] Undocumented individuals are prohibited from purchasing coverage in the exchange and therefore cannot receive premium credits.

[12] See https://www.healthcare.gov/glossary/special-enrollment-period/.

[13] This option is not likely for the self-employed with no employees who are not eligible to enroll in the SHOP.

Individuals who file their tax return as *single, married filing jointly, head of household,* or *qualifying widow/widower* may be eligible for the premium tax credit if they meet all the other criteria. Individuals filing *married filing separately* are not eligible for the premium tax credit with one exception. To qualify for the exception, a taxpayer must live apart from his or her spouse for at least six months of the year, file a separate return, maintain a household that is the residence of a dependent child for more than half the year, and provide more than half the cost of that household for the taxable year. In recent regulations, however, the IRS recognized that victims of domestic violence may not be able to meet this exception; therefore, it provided relief for 2014 and subsequent years for victims of domestic violence who meet the requirements outlined in IRS notice 2014-23 so they can file *married filing separately* and still receive a premium tax credit.[14]

Taxpayers who file a *married filing jointly* return who seek tax credits for only one spouse shall be treated as purchasing self-only coverage as long as they are not claiming a dependent under IRC Section 151.

AMOUNT OF THE CREDIT

The amount of the premium tax credit available is based on an individual's

- modified adjusted gross income,
- family size, and
- benchmark premium within each locality.

Based on one's income level and family size, an individual is required to contribute a certain percent of MAGI toward the premium. This is called the maximum percent premium contributions (see table 1-7). Therefore, the formula used to determine what share of premiums is taken as a tax credit is

Premium Tax Credit = Benchmark Premium − (MAGI × (maximum allowable percent contribution))

The tax credit subsidizes the remaining share of premiums greater than the maximum percent premium contribution amount. The higher one's MAGI, the higher the percent of his or her income that he or she must contribute to his or her health insurance premiums. For example, in 2016, households are required to contribute 9.66 percent of their MAGI toward premiums if their MAGI exceeds 300 percent (but is less than 400 percent) of the federal poverty level. It is less likely that households in this income level will receive a premium credit unless they have a large family and therefore are allowed a larger income threshold.

---

[14] Domestic abuse is defined to include physical, psychological, sexual, or emotional abuse, including efforts to control, isolate, humiliate, and intimidate, or to undermine the victim's ability to reason independently. All facts and circumstances are considered in determining whether an individual is abused.

Table 1-7 Maximum Percent Premium Contribution

Income as a Share of FPL	Share of Household Income Required		
	2015	2016	2017
100%	2.01%	2.03%	2.04%
132.9%	2.01%	2.03%	2.04%
133%	3.02%	3.05%	3.06%
150%	4.02%	4.07%	4.08%
200%	6.34%	6.41%	6.43%
250%	8.10%	8.18%	8.21%
300%	9.56%	9.66%	9.69%
350%	9.56%	9.66%	9.69%
400%	9.56%	9.66%	9.69%

Monthly Calculation

The determination of the premium credit amount is done monthly. A coverage month refers to a month in which the applicable taxpayer paid for coverage offered through the exchange and is not eligible for other minimum essential coverage.

Benchmark Premium

The premium level that is eligible for the credit is based on the second-lowest-cost "silver" plan in a geographic rating area in which the taxpayer resides. A silver plan reimburses, on average, 70 percent of covered health care expenses, with the remaining 30 percent paid out of pocket. Though a silver plan generally has higher premiums and lower copays and deductibles than the lower-tiered bronze plans, it has lower premiums and higher copays and deductibles than the higher-tiered platinum and gold plans. Benchmark premiums vary by state, county, age, gender, and whether an individual smokes.[15]

For illustration purposes, table 1-6 shows some examples of how the premium tax credit works for different income levels. The premium tax credit subsidy declines sharply for those with income more than 200 percent of FPL. For example, married couples with MAGI equal to 200 percent of the FPL receive, on average, tax credits to subsidize 69 percent of total premiums. Married couples with MAGI equal to 300 percent of the FPL receive tax credits to subsidize 30 percent of total premiums.

---

[15] See the following link for information about the second lowest cost silver plan https://www.cms.gov/cciio/resources/fact-sheets-and-faqs/downloads/second-lowest-cost-silver-plan-technical-faqs12162016.pdf.

TIMING OF TAX CREDIT

The tax credit is filed on a self-employed individual's federal tax return and is *advanceable*, meaning tax filers can choose to get the credit in advance to assist in paying health insurance premiums for the upcoming year. When a self-employed individual files taxes for the year in which he or she purchased health insurance, any differences more than or less than the advanceable amount will be reconciled (see table 1-8).

If an individual chooses not to receive the credit in advance, he or she can pay the premiums out of pocket and claim the full amount of the tax credit when filing the next tax return. This will either increase the refund or lower the balance due. The tax credit is considered "refundable," so that if the credit amount is greater than the individual's tax liability, he or she will receive a refund of this difference.

Table 1-8 Illustration: Share of Premiums Subsidized by Tax Credit by Income Level and Marital Status in 2015

Household Income Relative to Poverty Level	Maximum Premium Contribution Percentage (Relative to Income)	Maximum Monthly Premium Paid by Tax Filer	Monthly Premiums Subsidized by Tax Credit	Share of Premiums Subsidized with Tax Credits
Single				
100%	2.01%	$ 20	$248	93%
133%	3.02%	$ 39	$229	85%
150%	4.02%	$ 59	$209	78%
200%	6.34%	$123	$145	54%
250%	8.10%	$197	$ 71	26%
300%	9.56%	$279	$ 0	0%
350%	9.56%	$325	$ 0	0%
400%	9.56%	$372	$ 0	0%
Married				
100%	2.01%	$ 26	$510	95%
133%	3.02%	$ 53	$483	90%
150%	4.02%	$ 79	$457	85%
200%	6.34%	$166	$370	69%
250%	8.10%	$265	$270	50%
300%	9.56%	$376	$160	30%
350%	9.56%	$439	$ 97	18%
400%	9.56%	$501	$ 35	6%

Source: Estimates by Janemarie Mulvey and reprinted with permission from: *Health Reform: What Small Businesses Need to Know Now!*

Note: Estimates based on U.S. average annual benchmark premium of $3,215 single and $6,431 married in 2015 for 40-year-old non-smokers. Actual benchmark premiums will vary by locality.

KNOWLEDGE CHECK

6. Which variable is NOT part of the calculation of premium tax credit an individual might receive?

    a. Taxable income.

    b. Benchmark premium within each locality.

    c. Family size.

    d. Maximum allowed percent premium contribution.

Reconciliation of Premium Credits

Under the ACA, the amount received in premium credits is based on the prior year's income tax returns. Therefore, premium tax credits are advanceable and paid to the insurer prior to you filing your federal income tax return. These amounts are reconciled when individuals file tax returns for the actual year in which they receive premium credits.

When it is time to file a tax return, tax preparers must complete Form 8962, Premium Tax Credit (PTC), to reconcile advance credit premium tax credit payments with the PTC as calculated on the form. The completed Form 8962 must be filed with the taxpayer's federal income tax return.

If a tax filing unit's income decreases during the tax year, and the filer should have received a larger credit, this additional credit amount will be included in the tax refund for the year. On the other hand, any excess amount that was overpaid in premium credits will have to be repaid to the federal government as a tax payment. However, the ACA imposes limits on the excess amounts to be repaid for households with MAGI less than 400 percent at the time they file their taxes. As shown in table 1-10, the law includes specific limits that apply to single versus joint filers.

Individuals who purchased coverage through the Health Insurance Marketplace will receive annually a Form 1095-A, *Health Insurance Marketplace Statement* from their marketplace by early February. This form provides information they will need when completing Form 8962. If they have questions about the information on Form 1095-A for 2016 or about receiving Form 1095-A for 2017, they should contact their Marketplace directly. The IRS will not be able to answers questions about the information on a Form 1095-A or about missing or lost forms.

Table 1-9 Limits on Repayment of Excess Premium Credits

Modified Adjusted Gross Income Relative to FPL	Joint Filer	Single Filer
Less than 200% FPL	$600	$300
200%, but less than 300%, FPL	$1,500	$750
300%, but less than 400%, FPL	$2,500	$1,250

Source: IRS, Form 8962 Instructions at https://www.irs.gov/pub/irs-pdf/i8962.pdf

CHANGE IN CIRCUMSTANCES

Individuals are to report income and family size changes to the marketplace throughout the year. Reporting changes will help make sure they get the proper type and amount of financial assistance that will help them avoid getting too much or too little in advance. Receiving too much or too little in advance can affect their refund or balance due when you file your tax return.

For example, if they do not report income or family size changes to the marketplace when they happen, the advance payments may not match the actual qualified credit amount on the federal tax return. This might result in a smaller refund or a balance due.

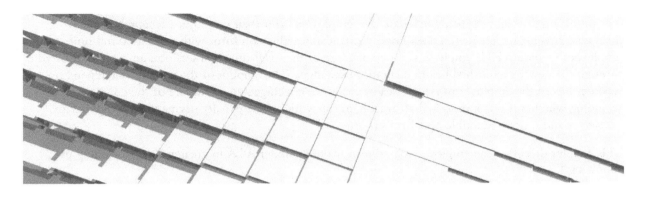

Chapter 2

EMPLOYER SHARED-RESPONSIBILITY PAYMENTS

LEARNING OBJECTIVES

After completing this chapter, you should be able to do the following:

- Estimate firm size based on full-time equivalents (FTEs) to determine which firms are potentially liable for an employer shared responsibility payment.
- Recall the correct definition of dependent for dependent coverage under the employer-shared responsibility payments.
- Identify what factors trigger an employer shared responsibility payment.
- Calculate potential penalties for employers who currently provide health insurance coverage and for those who do not provide health insurance coverage.
- Identify how potential penalties are applied in a controlled group.

INTRODUCTION

Employer-sponsored coverage remains an important source of health insurance for 68 percent of working adults.[1] To ensure that employers continue to provide some degree of health insurance coverage, the Patient Protection and Affordable Care Act (ACA) includes a shared-responsibility provision.[2]

---

[1] Fronstin, Paul, Sources of Health Insurance and Characteristics of the Uninsured: Analysis of the March 2013 Current Population Survey, Employee Benefit Research Institute, September 2013.
[2] Section 1513 of ACA-enacted IRC Section 4980(H).

The provision does not explicitly mandate that employers offer their employees acceptable health insurance coverage. However, it does impose financial penalties on firms with at least 50 full-time employees including FTE employees, if one or more of their full-time workers obtains a premium credit through the newly established health insurance exchanges. The amount of the penalty will depend on whether or not the employer provided health insurance coverage and the nature of the coverage, including whether it was considered affordable to the worker. The penalty payment is considered an excise tax and is not deductible on a firm's taxes.

This chapter discusses the employer-shared responsibility under ACA in greater detail, including the following:[3]

- Effective dates of potential penalties by firm size
- The three steps of estimating potential penalties:
  — Methodologies to calculate firm size
  — Identification of factors that trigger a penalty
  — Determinants of the penalty amount
- IRS notices
- Interaction of Medicaid expansion in certain states

---

[3] The IRS, in consultation with the Department of Health and Human Services and the Department of Labor, has issued final regulations on *Shared Responsibility for Employers Regarding Health Coverage*, see Federal Register Vol. 79, No. 29, February 12, 2014.

Effective Dates of Employer Shared-Responsibility Payments

The ACA states that the employer shared-responsibility payments would take effect January 1, 2014. There have, however, been a number of delays in the implementation date. As of the publication of this course, employers with 100 or more FTEs are potentially subject to a penalty effective January 1, 2015.

Employers who employ on average at least 50, but fewer than 100, FTEs have been provided transitional relief for all of 2015 for calendar year plans. The effective date for calendar year employers is January 1, 2016. However, the effective date will vary for employers with non-calendar year plans. (See table 2-1.) Firms with non-calendar year plans must have had those plans in place since December 12, 2012.

Table 2-1 Effective Dates for Employers With Non-Calendar Year Plans and 50 to 99 FTEs	
Plan Year	**Effective Dates**
April 1, 2015	April 1, 2016
July 1, 2015	July 1, 2016
Nov. 1, 2015	Nov. 1, 2016

In order to qualify for this transitional relief, employers with 50 to 99 FTEs must certify the following to the IRS for the period February 9, 2014, to December 31, 2014:[4]

- The employer did not reduce the size of its workforce or overall hours of service of employees unless for a *bona fide business reason.*
- The employer did not eliminate or materially reduce the health coverage it offered during this time period.[5]
- The employer did not alter the terms of the group coverage to narrow or reduce the class or classes of employees to whom coverage under those plans was offered on February 9, 2014.

---

[4] This information is to be reported as part of employer's 1094-C IRS information reports. Employers with 50 to 99 FTEs had to file their 1094-C information reports in 2016 for calendar year 2015 even though they were not liable for potential penalties in 2015.

[5] If there is a change in benefits under the employee-only coverage, the employer must certify that coverage provided MV (for example, had an AV of 60 percent).

The ACA Employer Shared-Responsibility Formula

The ACA employer shared-responsibility payment formula can be viewed in three distinct steps. The first step of the formula determines which firms are potentially subject to the penalty; the second step specifies which circumstances trigger the penalty payment; and the third step provides a formula for calculating the amount of the penalty.

Step 1 calculates whether an employer is considered an *applicable large employer* and therefore potentially subject to a penalty. The firm size measure is based on the number of FTEs, which includes some part-time workers but not certain seasonal ones. If the company does not have more than 50 FTEs, it will not pay a penalty, and the remainder of this chapter does not pertain to it.

Step 2 of the employer shared-responsibility formula specifies how a potential penalty can be triggered. Just because a firm makes it to step 2 does not mean the firm is automatically liable for a penalty. A penalty can only be triggered if one of the firm's full-time workers is eligible for a premium credit in the newly established health insurance exchange (also called health insurance marketplaces) because the worker's household income was lower than certain thresholds and the employer did not offer adequate and affordable health insurance coverage.

Step 3 calculates the amount of the penalty. The amount will depend on whether the employer currently provides health insurance coverage and the nature of the coverage offered.

STEP 1: DETERMINATION OF FIRM SIZE

The first part of the formula determines firm size by calculating the number of FTEs. FTEs equal the number of full-time employees and an FTE calculation based on the number of hours worked by part-time employees as a monthly average over a full year. Under the ACA, an applicable large employer is defined as an employer who employed *an average of at least 50 FTEs* on business days during the preceding *calendar year*. Note this is a calendar year calculation and not a plan year. Beginning in 2016, firms must use a 12-month average FTE count from the prior year to determine their firm size.

The potential employer penalty applies to all common law employers, including an employer that is a government entity (such as federal, state, local, or Indian tribal government entities), and an employer that is a nonprofit organization exempt from federal income taxes.

This section defines who is an employee (versus an independent contractor) and which employees are included in the FTE calculation. This section also includes a description of the IRS methodology for the determination of hours worked for workers who are not paid on an hourly basis.

Definition of an Employee

The ACA definition of an employee is based on the common law standard enforced by the IRS, which states that "anyone who performs services for you is your employee if you can control what will be done and how it will be done." [6] Therefore, the following are not considered *employees* for purposes of calculating the FTE:

- Leased employees
- Sole proprietor

---

[6] See www.irs.gov/Businesses/Small-Businesses-&-Self-Employed/Employee-Common-Law-Employee.

- Partner in a partnership
- Two-percent S-corporation shareholder
- Real estate agents and direct sellers[7]

Independent Contractors. Some employers incorrectly assume they can convert all of their employees into independent contractors to reduce their firm size calculation and avoid the penalty. The IRS makes clear distinctions between employees and independent contractors. According to the IRS, "the general rule is that an individual is an independent contractor if the payer has the right to control or direct only the result of the work and not what will be done and how it will be done."[8]

Leased Employees. The IRS guidance relating to the ACA also distinguishes between leased employees and an employee of the firm. Specifically, a leased worker is not an employee of the firm he or she is *leased* to but rather an employee of the temporary agency that actually pays him or her. Therefore, employees of temporary agencies are considered their employees for purposes of the FTE calculation and not the employee of the company who is *leasing* them.[9]

Part-Time Workers. The hours of part-time workers are used to determine firm size through the conversion of an FTE. Both full-time and part-time employees are included in the overall FTE calculation. Under the ACA law, a *full-time* employee is defined as one having worked on average at least 30 hours per week. Hours worked by part-time employees (that is, those working fewer than 30 hours per week) are converted into FTEs and are included in the calculation used to determine whether a firm is a large employer. Because employers determine average annual firm size based on monthly estimates, overall hours worked by part-time employees during a month are added up, and the total is divided by 120 and added to the number of full-time employees to get the number of FTE workers.

A potential source of confusion is that later when the penalty amount is determined, part-time workers cannot trigger the penalty and are not included in the penalty calculation. (See table 2-2.)

Seasonal Employees. Seasonal workers are generally taken into account in determining the number of FTEs. However, if an employer's workforce exceeds 50 full-time employees (including full-time equivalents) for 120 days or fewer during a calendar year, and the employees in excess of 50 who were employed during that period of no more than 120 days were seasonal workers, the employer is not considered an applicable large employer. Seasonal workers are workers who perform labor or services on a seasonal basis as defined by the secretary of the Department of Labor, and include retail workers employed exclusively during holiday seasons. According to the IRS, seasonal workers do not include staff at educational institutions. For this purpose, according to IRS guidance, employers may apply a reasonable, good faith interpretation of the term *seasonal worker* (table 2-2).

TRICARE or Veterans Administration Coverage. Employees who have coverage under a TRICARE or a Veterans Administration health program are not taken into account in determining if an employer is an applicable large employer (ALE). However, if this employee is working full-time than they are counted as full-time for purposes of estimating a penalty under step 3.

---

[7] IRC Section 3508.

[8] See www.irs.gov/Businesses/Small-Businesses-&-Self-Employed/Independent-Contractor-Defined.

[9] Note the treatment of leased workers in the employer-shared responsibility provisions is different from the Small Business Health Insurance Tax Credit where employers include leased employees from temporary agencies in their FTE calculation to determine eligibility for Small Business Health Insurance Tax Credit if they are employed for at least a year.

Table 2-2 Determination and Potential Application of Employer Penalty for Categories of Employees

Employee category	Calculation of FTE for Purposes of Determining if Large Employer	Triggers Penalty if Employee Received Premium Credit
Full-time	Counted as one employee, based on a 30-hour or more work week	Yes
Part-time	Prorated (divided by 120 to get monthly FTE)	No
Seasonal	Counted unless the inclusion of seasonal employees employed < 120 days (approximately four months) in a year is the only reason that FTE >50	Not considered full time if worked six months or less in a given year
Temporary Agency Employees	Generally counted as an employee of the temporary agency	Yes, for those employed by the temporary agency and who are determined to be full time, on average, for up to 12 months
TRICARE or Veteran's Administration Coverage	Not counted when determining FTE count	Most likely will not trigger penalty because has coverage, but is counted as a full-time employee for purposes of determining penalty amount

Source: Reprinted with permission from *Health Reform: What Small Businesses Need to Know Now!,* by Janemarie Mulvey, PhD.

Simplified Example of FTE Calculation

For example, consider a retail store with 45 full-time employees (30 or more hours). Assume the firm also has 40 part-time employees who all work 24 hours per week (3840 hours per month). These part-time employees' hours would be treated as equivalent to 32 full-time employees for the month, based on the following calculation:

$$(40 \text{ employees} \times 24 \text{ hours}) \times 4 \text{ weeks}) \div 120 = 3840 \div 120 = 32$$

Therefore, in this example, if the firm had the number of full-time and FTEs for all 12 months, the firm would be considered a *large employer*, based on a total FTE count of 77—that is, 45 full-time employees plus 32 FTEs based on the number of part-time hours worked. (See table 2-3.)

Table 2-3 Worksheet to Calculate FTE Monthly Average

Line Number	For Each Month Calculate the Following:	Your Firm	Example
1)	Number of FT employees*	_____	45
2)	Total PT Employees	_____	40
3)	Hours Worked Per Month for PT Employees	_____	96
4)	Total PT Hours Per Month (Line 2 × Line 3)	_____	3840
5)	Line 4 ÷ 120 to get FTE per month	_____	32
6)	Line 1 + Line 5 to get total FTE (including FT)	_____	77
7)	Calculate FTE for each month and add annual total here	_____	924
8)	Line 7 ÷ Line12 to get monthly FTE average	_____	77

*Full-time employees are defined as working 30 hours or more a week. See the following section on monthly measurement and look-back measurement methods to determine full-time.

Employers of Multiple Entities

The ACA also specifies how an employer of multiple entities (such as a franchise owner with several restaurants) is treated with respect to the calculation of FTEs. Specifically, the ACA follows the IRS aggregation rules governing *controlled groups*. That means if one individual or entity owns (or has a substantial ownership interest in) several companies, all of those companies are essentially considered one entity. In this case, for purposes of the 50 or more FTE rule, the employees in each of the jointly owned companies must be aggregated to determine the number of FTEs for the group as a whole. In this situation, each company is referred to as an applicable large employer *member*. However, noted as follows, the actual penalty is triggered and calculated within each entity.

Definition of Hours of Service

An hour of service is defined as an hour for which an employee is paid, or entitled to payment, for the performance of duties for the employer, and each hour for which an employee is paid or entitled to payment by the employer for a period of term during which no duties are performed due to vacation, holiday, illness, incapacity (including disability), layoff, jury duty, military duty, or leave of absence.

Calculating hours of service is straightforward for employees paid on an hourly basis. However, some employees are not compensated on an hourly basis, making it more difficult to determine their hours of services for purposes of calculating the FTE firm size number. The IRS has proposed that for employees paid on a non-hourly basis (such as salaried employees), an employer may calculate the actual hours of service using one of the following three methods:

- Same method as hourly workers, which is direct measurement by recording arrival and departure times
- Days-worked equivalency crediting the worker with eight hours of service for each day worked
- Weeks-worked equivalency crediting an employee with 30 hours of service for each week worked

An employer may apply different methods of calculating a non-hourly employee's hours of service for different categories of non-hourly employees.

Categories of Workers Excluded from Hours of Service Calculation

There are a number of categories of workers whose hours of service are not included in the FTE calculation. They are

- volunteer employees (including volunteer firefighters and emergency medical personnel),[10]
- unpaid students and interns (with the exception of the federal work study program), and
- members of religious orders.[11]

Adjunct Faculty. Under current guidance from the IRS, employers of adjunct faculty must account for hours worked in a *reasonable* manner and cannot simply count only the hours spent teaching a class each week as the actual number of hours worked. The IRS proposes one method (which is optional) to be an adjunct faculty member should be credited for each hour of teaching per week the following number of hours:

- Two hours and 15 minutes of service (representing a combination of teaching or classroom time and time performing related tasks such as class preparation and grading of examinations or paper)
- One hour of service for each additional hour outside of the classroom the faculty member spends performing duties he or she is required to perform (such as required office hours or required attendance at faculty meetings).

This equals *3.25 hours per week for each hour of teaching* assuming the faculty members only have one additional hour per week for the preceding second category.

Categories of Workers with Limited IRS Guidance. There are a number of categories of workers whose hours of service are particularly challenging to identify or track. The U.S. Treasury Department and the IRS continue to consider additional rules for the determination of hours of service for certain categories of employees, including commissioned salespeople and airline employees and certain categories of work hours associated with some positions of employment, including layover hours (for example for airline employees) and on-call hours. For this purpose, until further guidance is issued, employers are required to use a reasonable method of crediting hours of service that is consistent with section 4980H.[12] According to the IRS, a method of crediting hours is not reasonable if it takes into account only a portion of an employee's hours of service with the effect of characterizing, as a non-full-time employee, an employee in a position that traditionally involves at least 30 hours of service per week.

---

[10] This includes any volunteer who is an employee of a government entity or an organization described in Internal Revenue Code Section 501(c) that is exempt from taxation under Section 501(a) whose only compensation from that entity or organization is in the form of (i) reimbursement for (or reasonable allowance for) reasonable expenses incurred in the performance of services by volunteers, or (ii) reasonable benefits (including length of service awards), and nominal fees, customarily paid by similar entities in connection with the performance of service by volunteers.

[11] Until further guidance is issued.

[12] The preamble to the final regulations includes examples of methods of crediting these hours that are both reasonable and not reasonable, including a method that is considered reasonable for crediting hours of service for adjunct faculty members.

KNOWLEDGE CHECK

1. Which is considered an *employee* when calculating FTE to determine firm size?

    a. Part-time workers.

    b. Real estate agents and direct sellers.

    c. Independent contractors.

    d. Two-percent S corporation shareholder.

STEP 2: WHAT CONDITIONS TRIGGER A PENALTY?

Once an employer is considered large enough to be subject to a potential penalty, the second part of the formula determines whether the penalty is actually applied or *triggered*. However, not all employers with more than 50 FTEs are subject to a penalty.

Regardless of whether or not a company with 50 or more FTEs offers coverage, a penalty will be triggered only if at least one of its full-time employees obtains coverage through the newly established health insurance exchanges and receives a premium tax credit to subsidize the coverage. Full-time workers would be eligible for premium tax credits only if the following three conditions are met:

- Have household modified adjusted gross income between 100 percent and 400 percent of the federal poverty level (FPL) (400 percent of FPL equals $47,080 if single, $63,720 married with no children, and up to $97,000 for a family of four in 2016)[13]
- Are not eligible for coverage through a government-sponsored program like Medicaid or the Children's Health Insurance Program (CHIP)
- Are not eligible for coverage offered by an employer or are eligible only for employer coverage that is unaffordable or that does not provide minimum value (MV, also referred to as inadequate in this chapter)

It is important to note that a part-time worker (working less than 30 hours per week) cannot trigger the penalty even if he or she receives a premium credit in the exchange. The part-time worker is only included in the calculation of FTE for determining firm size.

---

[13] Eligibility for premium credits and amount of credit is tied to the Health and Human Services Poverty Guidelines for the prior year. Premium credits are available to individuals and households with income up to 400 percent of the federal poverty level.

KNOWLEDGE CHECK

2. Which type of workers cannot "trigger" a penalty if they enter the exchange and receive health insurance coverage?

    a. Seasonal workers who work full-time for more than six months.

    b. Full time workers.

    c. Part-time workers.

    d. Temporary agency employees determined to be full-time, on average, for up to 12 months.

STEP 3: CALCULATING THE EMPLOYER PENALTY

The actual amount of the penalty, once triggered, will vary depending on whether the employer currently offers health insurance coverage or not. If the employer offers coverage, that coverage must meet certain criteria with respect to affordability and adequacy (also called MV). If coverage is offered but inadequate or unaffordable, the penalty is generally limited to the number of *full-time workers* who enter the exchange and receive a premium credit. However, when the employer does not offer insurance coverage, if the penalty is triggered, it is applied to *all full-time employees* regardless of whether they have coverage elsewhere (for example, through a spouse, Medicare, or Medicaid).[14] The following discusses the components of the penalty calculation in greater detail.

Amount of Penalty if Employer Offers Inadequate or Unaffordable Coverage

To avoid a potential penalty, employers must offer health insurance coverage to at least 95 percent of their full-time employees and their dependents in 2016, and the coverage provided must be affordable and adequate. An employer's health plan is considered

- *affordable* when the worker's required contribution toward the plan premium for *self-only* coverage is less than or equal to 9.66 percent of his or her household income or[15]
- *adequate* (or meeting MV) if the health plan pays for at least 60 percent, on average, of covered health care expenses.

If one of their full-time workers (or their dependents) does not receive adequate or affordable coverage and obtains premium credits for coverage through the newly established exchanges, the employer will be penalized. If a penalty is triggered in this case, the monthly penalty assessed to an employer for each full-time employee who receives a premium credit is shown in table 2-4.

Offering a choice between two penalty amounts is important for firms who may have a large number of low-income employees who are eligible for premium credits if the firm's plans are deemed unaffordable (defined as follows). Under this scenario, the cost-effective alternative is to pay the fine of $2,000 (as adjusted for inflation) per full-time worker (divided by 12 to get monthly penalty) and subtracting 30 full-time workers. Otherwise, if the firm only has a handful of low-income workers who

---

[14] The one exception for the full-time worker count used in the penalty calculation is full-time seasonal workers. If the seasonal workers worked full-time for less than 120 days a year, they are not part of the count of full-time workers for purposes of determining the amount of the total penalty.

[15] This percent was initially 9.5 percent in 2014 and rises to 9.69 percent by 2017.

trigger the penalty, it may be more cost-effective to pay the higher amount of ($3,000 as adjusted for inflation) per low-income worker receiving a premium credit and also divided by 12 to a monthly penalty amount.[16]

<table>
<tr><td colspan="3">Table 2-4 Amount of Penalty if Health Insurance Coverage Offered is Inadequate or Unaffordable</td></tr>
<tr><td></td><td colspan="2">If Penalty is Triggered:</td></tr>
<tr><td>Firm Size</td><td>Amount in 2016</td><td>Amount in 2017</td></tr>
<tr><td>50 or more full-time employees including FTEs</td><td>Lesser of:
(# of Full-time workers who receive a premium credit) times $3,240
OR
(# of Full-time workers minus 30) times $2,160</td><td>Lesser of:
(# of Full-Time Employees who receive a premium credit) times $3,396
OR
((# of Full-Time Employees minus 30) times $2,264)</td></tr>
<tr><td colspan="3">Source: Federal Register, Vol. 79, No. 29, February 12, 2014.</td></tr>
</table>

It is important to point out that the $2,000 and $3,000 penalty amounts specified in the ACA statute are based on 2014 dollars. According to the ACA statute, the penalty amounts are adjusted annually based on the premium adjustment percentage after 2014.[17] Therefore, the 2016 employer penalties after indexing for inflation are $2,160 and $3,240.

KNOWLEDGE CHECK

3. Which worker is included in the calculation of FTEs for purposes of determining firm size in the employer-shared responsibility payments?

   a. Employees with TRICARE or VA coverage.
   b. Seasonal workers working more than 120 days.
   c. Real estate agents.
   d. Leased employees.

Dependent Coverage. As noted previously, in order to avoid a potential penalty, *applicable large employers* must offer coverage to 95 percent of their full-time employees and the full-time employees' dependents in 2016. *Dependent* is defined as a child of an employee who has not attained age 26.[18] Dependent children

---

[16] The penalty amounts of $2,000 and $3,000 are in 2014. In 2016, these amounts rise to $2,160 and $3,240 and to $2,264 and $3,396 with inflation adjustments.

[17] ACA Section 1302(c)(4).

[18] See IRC Section 152(f)(1).

under this definition is different than dependent children in other parts of the tax code and there is no requirement that the dependent currently resides with the parent nor does the parent have to claim them as a dependent on their taxes.[19] This includes the entire calendar month in which the child turns 26. The definition of dependent in the ACA statute does not include the spouse of the employee.

The definition of dependents includes biological children and adopted children, but excludes foster children and stepchildren (table 2-5). The dependent in this case does not have to reside with their parents and does not have to be claimed as a dependent on their parent's tax return. This definition of dependent also excludes a child who is not a U.S. citizen or national, unless that child is a resident of a country contiguous to the United States or within the exception of adopted children described in IRC Section 152(b)(3)(B). Absent knowledge to the contrary, applicable large employers may rely on an employee's representation about that employee's children and the ages of those children.

Table 2-5 Definition of Dependent

Relationship	Dependent
Biological Children (under age 26)	Yes
Adopted Children (under age 26)	Yes
Foster Children	No
Stepchildren	No
Spouse	No

Source: Federal Register, Vol. 79, No. 29, February 12, 2014.

Determining Whether Coverage is Affordable. Under the ACA, coverage under an employer-sponsored plan is affordable to a particular employee if the employee's required contribution for *self-only* coverage does not exceed 9.66 percent of the employee's household income in the 2016 taxable year.

Household income is defined as the modified adjusted gross income (MAGI) of the employee and any members of the employee's family (which would include any spouse and dependents) who are required to file an income tax return. MAGI is adjusted gross income plus certain foreign income and tax-exempt interest and under the ACA also includes the nontaxable portion of Social Security income.[20]

When the proposed regulation was first released, employers voiced their concerns that they do not have access to information regarding their workers' household income, let alone their MAGI. To address this concern and provide employers a more workable option for determining the affordability of their health insurance coverage, the Treasury and the IRS have proposed three *safe harbor* optional methods for determining whether the affordability provision is met using the wage information that is currently available to employers. An employer may choose to use one or more of these safe harbors for all of its employees or for any reasonable category of employees, provided it does so on a uniform and consistent basis for all employees in a category.

---

[19] Ibid.

[20] This definition of MAGI is similar to the definition of MAGI for ACA premium tax credits but different than other areas of the tax code, such as determining the individual shared responsibility payments under ACA.

If an employee's premium contributions for self-only coverage does not exceed 9.66 percent of the following safe harbor measures, the employer's plan is deemed affordable, and the employer will not be subject to a penalty:

- W-2 Safe Harbor: Amount of wages paid to the employee as reported in box 1 of that employee's current year Form W-2: Wage and Tax Statement. This amount excludes contributions to 401(k) plans and IRC Section 125 cafeteria plans.
- Rate of Pay Safe Harbor: An amount equal to 130 hours multiplied by the lower of the employee's hourly rate of pay as of the first day of the coverage period or the employee's lowest hourly rate of pay during the calendar year.[21]
- Federal Poverty Safe Harbor: An amount equal to the federal poverty level for single filers for a calendar year divided by 12. Allowed to use federal poverty guidelines in effect six months prior to the beginning of the plan year.[22]

KNOWLEDGE CHECK

4. Which is NOT considered a safe-harbor proxy for monthly household MAGI for purposes of the affordability criteria required by ACA?

   a. Annual federal poverty level.
   b. The worker's adjusted gross income.
   c. W-2 wage income.
   d. Hourly rate of pay multiplied by 130 hours.

Determining Whether Coverage is Adequate. Under the ACA, a plan is considered to provide adequate coverage (also called MV) if the plan covered, on average, 60 percent of the cost of covered benefits. The 60 percent threshold is also referred to as the actuarial value (AV) of the plan. The measure is an average, so it does not apply to one individual's insured experience, rather it is the average across all insured individuals. The remaining 40 percent of plan costs would be paid out of pocket. According to IRS guidance, employers will have to calculate the AV of their health plans using one of three potential approaches for determining whether an employer plan provides MV:[23]

- An AV calculator is available to employers from the Department of Health and Human Services: https://www.cms.gov/CCIIO/Resources/Regulations-and-Guidance/Downloads/2015-av-calculator-final.xlsm.
- An array of design-based safe harbors in the form of checklists that would provide a simple, straightforward way to ascertain that employer-sponsored plans provide MV with the need to perform any calculations or obtain the assistance of an actuary.
- For plans with nonstandard features that preclude the use of the AV calculator or the MV calculator without adjustments, an appropriate certification can be made by a certified actuary.

---

[21] The final regulations, unlike the proposed regulations, permit an employer to use the rate of pay safe harbor even if an hourly employee's hourly rate of pay is reduced during the year.

[22] Example using federal poverty level for single coverage = 9.66% × $11,770 = $1137/ 12 = $94.75 month. In this case, the employee's share of the premiums cannot exceed $94.75 per month.

[23] The MV regulation can be found at: Federal Register, Vol. 78, No. 86, May 8, 2013. www.gpo.gov/fdsys/pkg/ FR-2013-05-03/pdf/2013-10463.pdf. Additional guidance can be found at www.irs.gov/pub/irs-drop/n-14-69.pdf.

The AV calculation for determining MV includes the employer contributions to health savings accounts and health reimbursement accounts that are part of a high-deductible health plan.

Amount of Penalty if Employer Does Not Offer Insurance Coverage

The penalty can be significantly higher if the employer does not offer coverage at all and a full-time worker becomes eligible for premium credits in the exchange. When the employer does not offer insurance coverage, the penalty applied is $2,000 times the number of full-time workers in the firm. This increases reflecting inflation adjustments to $2,160 in 2016 and $2,264 in 2017. As noted earlier, the $2,000 inflation adjusted penalty is an annual penalty amount, but the actual penalty calculated per month and equal to $166.67 per month (= $2,000 ÷ 12). When calculated on a monthly basis, the number of full-time workers per month can vary (see the following measurement issues). It is important to note that although full-time workers receiving Medicare, Medicaid, or other coverage through a spouse are not eligible for premium credits in the exchange and therefore cannot trigger the penalty, they are included in the count of full-time workers on which the penalty is applied. However, firms are allowed to deduct 30 from the count of full-time workers in 2016 before applying the $2,160 per worker in 2016. (See table 2-6.)

Table 2-6 Amount of Penalty by Size of Employer That Does Not Offer Coverage and Full-Time Worker Qualifies for a Premium Credit

Firm Size	If Penalty is Triggered	
	Amount in 2016	Amount in 2017 and Thereafter
50 or more FTEs	(# of Full-time Employees – 30) × $2,160	(# of Full-Time Employees – 30) × $2,264

Source: Federal Register, Vol. 79, No. 29, February 12, 2014.

KNOWLEDGE CHECK

5. An employer with 150 full-time employees does not provide health insurance coverage in 2016 and 15 of its full-time workers become eligible for premium credits in the exchange. Twenty of the employer's full-time workers currently are eligible for Medicare. How much will the employer-shared responsibility payment be in 2016 including inflation adjustments to the penalty after 2014?

    a. $100,000.

    b. $259,200.

    c. $216,000.

    d. $140,000.

METHODOLOGY TO MEASURE NUMBER OF FULL-TIME WORKERS

Prior to the ACA, many employers knew which workers were considered full time and which were not. Now, however, the ACA defines full time as 30 hours a week, and the number of full-time workers in a given month is a key determinant of the total annual penalty an employer might owe. So, it is important for employers to have an accurate count of their full-time workers.[24]

To assist employers in this calculation, the IRS has provided details on various methodologies employers can use to estimate the number of full-time workers. However, the process can be confusing and complex. First of all, the potential employer penalty is derived from monthly estimates of full-time workers that are then aggregated over a 12-month period. This approach is different from the FTE calculation done earlier to determine firm size, which is based on an annual average. The definition of full time is still 30 hours a week for purposes of determining the penalty amount. Adding to the complexity, the formula for counting the number of full-time workers in a month is to divide the number of hours by 130 hours (instead of the 120 hours that were used for the FTE calculation).[25]

The methodology to measure full time is also important for accounting hours worked for variable-hour employees. These employees may appear to be part time in any one week but whose hours may vary widely from week to week.

The IRS has provided a definition of variable-hour employees. Under the IRS definition, a new employee is a *variable hour employee* if, based on the facts and circumstances at the start date, it cannot be determined that the employee is reasonably expected to be employed on average at least 30 hours per week.

In some cases, variable-hour employees may not work the necessary 30 hours on average over a specified time period (up to 12 months) to be considered full time. However, a new employee who is expected to be employed initially at least 30 hours per week may be a variable-hour employee if, based on the facts and circumstances at the start date, the period of employment at more than 30 hours per week is reasonably expected to be of limited duration.

Variable-hour employees also might not necessarily be considered full time during each week within a given month, but they would be considered full-time employees for the purposes of this calculation as long as they worked 130 hours over the entire month. This is an important issue for the hospitality, retail, construction, and restaurant industries in which work hours may vary depending on certain events, the weather, or other reasons.

The IRS has developed two safe harbor methodology options for employers to use to determine whether a new or ongoing variable-hour or seasonal worker is considered *full time* for purposes of calculating the total penalty owed.

- Monthly measurement method
- Look-back measurement method

---

[24] It is important to note that methodology for determining the number of full-time workers for step 3 to determine the amount of the penalty is different than determining the FTE calculation for step 1 discussed earlier.

[25] The reason for the difference is that the 130 hours is determined by regulation that used the formula: 30 hours × 52 weeks ÷ 12 = 130. Whereas, 120 hours for the FTE calculation was written in the actual ACA statute and cannot be changed without changes to the legislation.

Monthly Measurement Period

Under the monthly measurement method, an employer determines each employee's status as a full-time employee by counting the employee's hours of service for each calendar month. Under the monthly measurement method, an employer will not be subject to a penalty payment because of a failure to offer coverage to that employee before the end of the period of three full calendar months starting with the first full calendar month in which the employee is otherwise eligible for an offer of coverage in a group health plan. Under the monthly measurement method, an employee must be considered a continuing employee and not a new hire.[26] In addition, under this method, the special unpaid leave and employee break period rules do not apply.

There is an option for employers to use four- and five-week periods of measurement under this method. This option is referred to as the *weekly rule*. A week means any period of seven consecutive calendar days applied consistently by an employer for each calendar month. For calendar months using four-week periods, an employee with at least 120 hours of service is a full-time employee. For a calendar month using a five-week period, an employee with at least 150 hours of service is considered full time. This option is only applicable for counting full-time workers for employers who are not offering health insurance coverage. Those offering coverage must use a calendar month measurement.

Look-Back Measurement Method

A more complex but more thorough method is the look-back measurement approach that allows an employer to measure how many hours an employee averaged per week during a defined period of time (not less than three and not more than 12 consecutive months), called the measurement period. If an employee is determined to have worked full time during the measurement period, an employer will then have the option of entering an administrative period during which the employee may be enrolled in a health plan. Following the administrative period, the employee would be treated as a full-time employee during a stability period.

A penalty, if applicable, is incurred only during the *stability period* that lasts at least six consecutive calendar months and is no shorter in duration than the standard measurement period designated by the employer.

- If an employer determines that an employee did not work full time during the standard measurement period, the employer would not be required to treat the workers as full time during the subsequent stability period.
- If an employee was full time during the measurement period, then the employer could potentially pay a penalty during the stability period if all other criteria were met (for example, full-time employees entered the exchange and received a premium tax credit, and any health insurance coverage offered was not adequate or affordable).
- The full-time classification would remain in place during the stability period so long as the worker remained an employee, regardless of how many hours he or she worked during the stability period.

Employers may create different measurement and stability periods for different categories of employees. These periods can differ either in length or in their starting and ending dates for the following categories of ongoing employees:

- Collectively bargained and non-collectively bargained employees
- Salaried and hourly employees
- Employees of different entities (controlled groups)
- Employees located in different states

---

[26] This applies unless an employee has had a period of at least 13 weeks during which no hours of service were credited (26 weeks for an employee of an educational organization).

The rules also provide an option to use an *administrative period* (between the measurement and stability periods) to determine which ongoing employees are eligible for coverage and to notify and enroll employees in health care plans. However, any administrative period between the standard measurement period and stability period may neither reduce nor lengthen the measurement period or stability period. The administrative period following the standard measurement period may last up to 90 days and overlaps with the prior stability period to prevent any gaps in coverage.

Look-Back Measurement Methods for Different Groups of Workers

During this look-back period, the IRS defines how the measurement, administrative, and stability periods are determined for three groups of workers (figure 2-1 and table 2-7):

- Ongoing employees
- New employees: reasonably expected to work full time
- New employees: safe harbor for variable-hour and seasonal employees

Ongoing Employees

An ongoing employee is generally an employee who has been employed for at least one complete standard measurement period. This is a defined period of not less than three and not more than 12 consecutive months. Under the safe harbor method for ongoing employees, an employer determines each ongoing employee's status by looking back at the standard measurement period. According to the IRS, an employer has the flexibility to determine the months when the standard measurement period starts and ends, provided that the determination is made on a uniform and consistent basis for all employees in the same category. During this measurement period, the employer must first determine if the employee worked on average at least 30 hours per week per month.

Figure 2-1 Determining Whether an Employee is Full-Time Using the Look-Back Measurement Method

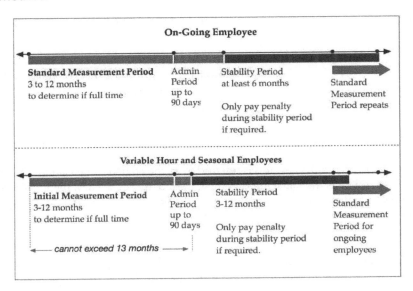

Source: Reprinted with permission from *Health Reform: What Small Businesses Need to Know Now!,* by Janemarie Mulvey. Based on guidance from IRS Notice 2012-58, *Determining Full-time Employees for Purposes of Shared Responsibility for Employers Regarding Health Insurance.*

If the employer determines that an employee averaged at least 30 hours per week during the standard measurement period, then the employer treats the employee as a full-time employee during a subsequent stability period, regardless of the number of hours the employee works during the stability period, so long as he or she remains an employee.

New Employees Reasonably Expected to Work Full Time. The easiest group to assess regarding full-time status are new employees that are reasonably expected to work full time. If an employee is reasonably expected at his or her start date to work full time, an employer that offers a group health plan will not face an ACA penalty if it covers new workers within three calendar months of their start date and that coverage meets the affordability and adequacy requirement described as follows. This provision applies to new workers who are expected to work full time.

Table 2-7 Time Frame for Determining Full-Time Status for Purposes of Applying Penalty

	Measurement Period	Administrative Period	Stability Period
Definition	Measure (on average) whether employees are full time or not	Identify and enroll full-time employees	Period in which penalty may be due relative to employees found to be full time during measurement period
Ongoing Employees	3 to 12 months[a]	Up to 90 days (may neither reduce nor lengthen the measurement or stability period—can overlap prior stability period)	At least 6 months, but cannot be shorter in duration than measurement period
New Employees Hired as Full Time	Not applicable	Up to 90 days to enroll	Not applicable
New Variable-Hour and Seasonal Employees	3 to 12 months[b]	Up to 90 days (measurement period and administrative period cannot exceed 13 months)[c]	3 to 12 months, but cannot be longer than measurement period

Source: Reprinted with permission from: *Health Reform: What Small Businesses Need to Know Now!*, by Janemarie Mulvey.
Table Notes: (a) For ongoing employees, this is referred to as the standard measurement period. (b) For new employees, this is referred to as the initial measurement period. (c) Technically, the initial measurement and administrative period cannot last beyond the final day of the first calendar month beginning on or after the one-year anniversary of the employee (about 13 months).

Variable-Hour and Seasonal Employees. IRS guidance allows employers to use an initial measurement period of three to 12 consecutive months (as selected by the employer) to determine whether new variable hour employees or seasonal employees are full-time. The employer measures the hours of service completed by the new employee during the initial measurement period and determines whether the employee completed an average of 30 hours of service per week or more during this period. If an employee is determined to be full time during the initial measurement period, the employer would have up to three months to enroll him or her in a health insurance plan. The initial measurement period and administrative period cannot last beyond the final day of the first calendar month beginning on or after the worker's one-year anniversary (about 13 months). For example, if an employer takes 12 months to measure whether workers are full time, the employer then has up to one month to enroll them in a plan. Similarly, if employers choose 10 months as the initial measurement period, they have three months to enroll them.

During this 13-month period, workers without coverage can enroll in the newly created health insurance exchanges where they may receive premium tax credits. Employers are not required to pay a penalty for this 13-month period. As noted previously, the penalty period begins only after the administrative period if the employer does not provide adequate and affordable coverage and at least one of its employees enters an exchange and receives a premium credit.

The definition of full time is based on the entire 12-month measurement period. So, if a variable-hour employee works full time some weeks and part time others, the total hours worked in the 12-month period divided by the number of weeks an employee works would result in the average number of hours worked per week.[27]

Definition of Seasonal Workers. The definition of seasonal worker differs across the two-part calculation used to determine the ACA employer penalty. Specifically, the seasonal worker definition varies depending on whether it is used in the first part of the calculation, which determines whether an employer is considered large (the 50-FTE calculation), or the second part of the calculation, which determines how many employees are considered full time for purposes of setting the dollar amount of the penalty.

For the first part of the calculation—determining whether a firm meets the ACA definition of an applicable large employer—if a seasonal employee works less than 120 days during a year (equivalent to about six months if working five-day weeks), he or she is not included in the FTE calculation. In this instance, the definition of a seasonal worker is not limited to agricultural or retail workers. For the second part of the calculation—seasonal workers are not considered full time if they are employed in a position for which the customary annual employment is six months or less. The period of employment should begin each calendar year in approximately the same part of the year (such as summer or winter). In certain unusual instances, the employee can be considered a seasonal employee even if the seasonal employment is extended in a particular year beyond its customary duration (regardless of whether the customary duration is six months or less than six months). For example, ski instructors who stay on because there is an unusually long or heavy snow season.

EFFECTIVE DATES FOR MEASUREMENT PERIODS

Firms with at least 50 and up to 99 FTEs who want to use the look-back measurement periods must start measuring in 2015 for an effective date of January 1, 2016, if they operate their health plans on a calendar year basis. The IRS and the Treasury recognize that employers who want to have a 12-month measurement period and a 12-month stability period may face constraints the first year. Therefore, the IRS is offering a *transitional measurement period* that can be (for the first year of implementation only) shorter than the stability period.

---

[27] Note that this method conforms to that described in step 1, in which the size of the firm is determined based on the number of full-time workers. It differs from that of step 3, in which the number of full-time workers is computed for each month during a given period to determine an applicable penalty, if any.

The IRS recognizes that these periods may differ depending on whether the employer's health plan or the firm's financial operations are based on a calendar or fiscal year. Also, the guidance states that employers who use a full 12-month measurement period are not required to begin the measurement period before July 1, 2015. (See example in table 2-8 for employer with fiscal year starting on November 1, 2015.) The IRS provides examples in its guidance of start and end dates for the measurement, administrative, and stability periods that meet requirements outlined in the final rule issued on February 12, 2014.

Table 2-8 Examples of Start and End Dates during Transition Period for Firms with 50 to 99 FTEs

Plan Year	Transitional Measurement Period	Administrative Period	Stability Period
Calendar Year	April 15, 2015–Oct. 14, 2015	Oct. 15, 2015–Dec. 31, 2015	Jan. 1, 2016–Dec. 31, 2016
Fiscal Year Starting On			
April 1, 2016	July 1, 2015–Dec. 31, 2015	Jan. 1, 2016–March 31, 2016	April 1, 2016–March 31, 2017
July 1, 2016	June 15, 2015–April 14, 2016	April 15, 2016–June 30, 2016	July 1, 2016–July 1, 2017
Nov. 1, 2016	Sept. 1, 2015–Aug. 31, 2016	Sept. 1, 2016–Oct. 31, 2016	Nov. 1, 2016–Nov. 1, 2017

Source: Reprinted with permission from: *Health Reform: What Small Businesses Need to Know Now!*, by Janemarie Mulvey.
Note: An employer with a FY beginning on July 1, 2016, must use a measurement period that is longer than six months to comply with the required measurement period beginning by no later than July 1, 2015, and ending no earlier than 90 days before the stability period.

CALCULATION OF PENALTY FOR CONTROLLED GROUPS

The actual penalty is only applicable to full-time workers, and each group within the controlled group has to individually calculate a potential penalty. In doing this, each entity of the controlled group would use their respective count of full-time employees and insurance coverage characteristics. Therefore, each entity can subtract 30 adjusted by their share of full time workers from their count of full-time workers depending on the year in which they calculate the penalty. The insurance coverage they offer can differ across entities of the controlled group and the adequacy and affordability tests are tested separately for each entity within the controlled group.

Government Entities and Churches. The latest regulatory guidance in February 2014 states that the final regulations continue to reserve on the application of the employer aggregation rules under the IRC controlled group rules (IRC Section 414(b), (c), M, and (o)) to government entities, as well as to churches or conventions or associations of churches. Until further guidance is issued, those entities may apply a reasonable good faith interpretation of the controlled group rules in determining their status as an applicable large employer.

KNOWLEDGE CHECK

6. Which statement is NOT accurate concerning the application of the employer-shared responsibility payments for controlled groups?

    a. The determination of ALE Status (in other words, firm size) is based on the aggregate FTE count across all members of the controlled group.
    b. The determination of the penalty amount is based on the characteristics of each entity of the controlled group is levied separately for each.
    c. The determination of ALE status (in other words, firm size) is based on the FTE count of each individual entities of a controlled group.
    d. The penalty is triggered by an individual entity of the controlled group. Therefore it applies only to that member.

PENALTY LIABILITY AND IRS REPORTING REQUIREMENTS

If one or more of a firm's employees receives a premium tax credit or cost-sharing reduction, the IRS will contact employers to inform them of their potential liability and provide them an opportunity to respond before any liability is assessed or notice and demand for payment is made. The IRS will issue further guidance in this area.

Employers should not expect to see a notice from the IRS until after April 15, 2016, as they will first have to reconcile the employee's premium tax credits with the employee's tax records, and information returns from the companies have to have been submitted, which are not due until March 1, 2016.

Any assessable payment under IRC Section 4980H is payable upon notice and demand and is assessed and collected in the same manner as Subchapter B of Chapter 68 of the Tax Code. It is considered an excise tax and so is not tax deductible.

Interaction between Medicaid Expansions and Potential Employer Penalties

The ACA included a provision for states to expand their Medicaid program to lower-wage workers (including those making the minimum wage). Traditionally, state Medicaid programs have provided subsidized health insurance coverage to lower-income pregnant women, the disabled, and children.[28] The new health care reform law allows states to voluntarily expand subsidized Medicaid coverage to workers earning the minimum-wage and less with household income up to 138 percent of the poverty level ($16,478 for single individuals in 2016). The employer penalty is not triggered if a full-time worker chooses to enroll in the newly expanded Medicaid program.

The Medicaid expansion to nontraditional households under the ACA is voluntary, and the federal government cannot mandate that states activate this option.[29] As seen in figure 2-2, 19 states have chosen not to expand their Medicaid program, as of January 1, 2017.[30] This has important implications for any small business whose workforce includes a large share of minimum-wage workers. In states that choose not to expand Medicaid, most uninsured minimum-wage workers would be eligible for premium tax credits to purchase insurance in the newly established health insurance exchanges. However, there may be some workers whose income is less than 100 percent of FPL and not eligible for premium credits in the exchange (referred to as the coverage gap).

More importantly, in states that do not expand Medicaid, minimum wage-workers offer unique challenges to small businesses, especially in light of employer penalties. Smaller firms are more likely to employ lower-wage and minimum-wage workers than their larger competitors.[31] Minimum-wage workers are concentrated in the service sector, with the vast majority working in restaurants and other food services.

Whether a full-time minimum wage worker enrolls in either Medicaid or the exchange has important implications for the employer penalty discussed previously. Specifically, full-time minimum or low wage workers who are eligible to enroll in Medicaid do not trigger an employer penalty. But in states that have not voluntarily expanded Medicaid, those employers could be penalized if their full-time workers instead become eligible for premium tax credits and enroll in the individual exchanges. (See figure 2-2.)

From a total compensation perspective, firms that pay workers the minimum wage cannot readily adjust money wages downward to pay potential penalties for not providing health insurance coverage without jeopardizing their profitability. This could adversely affect small businesses in those states that have not voluntarily expanded their Medicaid programs under the ACA.

---

[28] Medicaid is funded jointly by the federal government and individual states. Medicaid expansions under the ACA are paid for largely through the federal government in the early years of implementation.

[29] On June 28, 2012, the Supreme Court ruled on *National Federation of Independent Business v. Sebelius* (NFIB) that a state can refuse to participate in the ACA Medicaid expansion without losing any of its current federal Medicaid matching funds.

[30] Kaiser Family Foundation, *Status of State Actions on Medicaid Expansions.*

[31] Blumberg, Linda J. and Stacey McMorrow, *What Would Health Care Reform Mean for Small Employers and Their Workers?* Timely Analysis of Immediate Health Policy Issues, Robert Wood Johnson Foundation and the Urban Institute, December 2009.

Current Status of State Medicaid Expansion Decisions

Figure 2-2 Current Status of State Medicaid Expansion Decisions, as of January 1, 2017

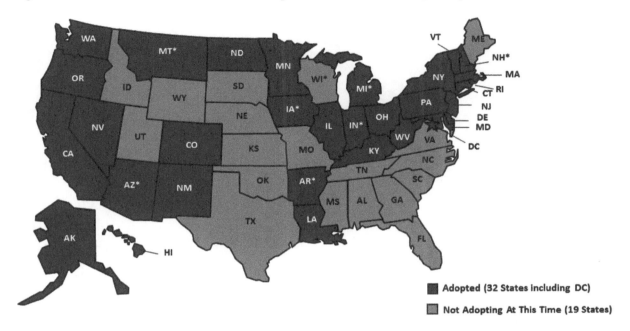

Adopted (32 States including DC)

Not Adopting At This Time (19 States)

NOTES: Current status for each state is based on KCMU tracking and analysis of state executive activity. *AR, AZ, IA, IN, MI, MT, and NH have approved Section 1115 waivers. WI covers adults up to 100% FPL in Medicaid, but did not adopt the ACA expansion.
SOURCE: "Status of State Action on the Medicaid Expansion Decision," KFF State Health Facts, updated January 1, 2017.
http://kff.org/health-reform/state-indicator/state-activity-around-expanding-medicaid-under-the-affordable-care-act/

Source: Kasier Family Foundation, *Status of State Actions on Medicaid Expansions.* pp

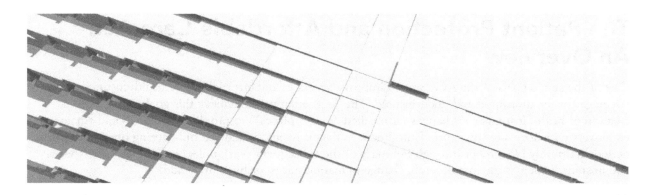

Chapter 3

IRS EMPLOYER AND INSURER REPORTING REQUIREMENTS

LEARNING OBJECTIVES

After completing this chapter, you should be able to do the following:

- Identify the Patient Protection and Affordable Care Act (ACA) provisions that the IRS is responsible for in terms of implementation, administration, and enforcement.
- Identify which IRS reporting forms and required information employers and insurers must submit.
- Identify what elements are to be reported on IRS ACA reporting.
- Recall due dates for IRS reporting requirements.
- Identify under which circumstances a firm can use the general versus alternative method of reporting.

The Patient Protection and Affordable Care Act: An Overview

One of the stated goals of the ACA was to improve access to and affordability of health insurance coverage for the uninsured and underinsured. The ACA attempts to achieve this goal through the creation of health insurance exchanges (also called "marketplaces") to provide individuals and small employers with access to insurance. Enrollment in the exchanges is allowed only during open enrollment periods (currently November through February of the subsequent year), unless individuals have special circumstances such as the loss of a job, change in marital status, or birth of a child.

Although the exchanges help improve access to health insurance coverage, this coverage may still not be affordable to lower-income individuals and their families. To improve affordability, the ACA provides subsidies in the form of premium tax credits to lower-income individuals to purchase insurance coverage on the exchanges.

The ACA also includes *shared-responsibility* payments for employers and individuals. Under the employer shared-responsibility provision, employers with 50 or more full-time equivalent (FTE) employees may potentially pay a penalty if one of their full-time employees enrolls in the newly established individual exchanges and receives a premium tax credit. Their employees would be eligible only for a premium credit if the employer did not offer insurance or the insurance that was offered did not meet certain guidelines. The intent of the employer shared-responsibility payment was to provide some financial incentive for large employers to maintain current health insurance coverage. The shared-responsibility payment is complex to administer and has caused a great deal of confusion especially among smaller firms.

Under the individual shared-responsibility payments (also called individual mandates), most uninsured Americans will have to buy insurance or pay a fine that varies by income level. The intent of the individual mandate is to encourage all individuals to obtain health insurance coverage when available and not wait until they may become seriously ill, which could raise the average premium of care for all enrollees.

ACA Requirements for IRS Information Reports and other Employee Notifications

The IRS is responsible for implementation, administration, and enforcement of employer and individual penalties, as well as premium tax credits for small businesses and individuals. In order to do this, the IRS is authorized to collect information reports from affected entities. As a result, employers with 50 or more FTEs are required to submit information reports to the IRS and to each full-time worker in 2017 describing the nature of their insurance coverage or lack thereof during the 2016 plan year. Insurers are also required to document the provision of minimum essential coverage to workers and to the IRS through a separate return.

This chapter discusses the information reporting requirements in terms of effective dates and potential penalties for not reporting. Then for each entity (for example, employers and insurers) the chapter will discuss the detailed elements required to be reported, including special considerations for multiemployer plans, controlled groups, and government entities.

In addition, the ACA requires two other employer reporting requirements:

- An additional reporting requirement on a worker's W-2 Form regarding the total value of health insurance coverage provided by the employer
- A disclosure requirement to workers regarding availability of exchanges and interaction between exchanges and employer provided coverage

These two additional requirements are discussed in greater detail at the end of this chapter.

IRS REPORTING REQUIREMENTS

The ACA requires that employers and insurers report to the IRS and directly to their workers information regarding the existence and nature of health insurance coverage. This information will be used to administer and enforce the employer shared-responsibility provisions and to ensure that individuals meet the requirements of minimum essential coverage under the ACA's individual mandate. In addition, this information will be used to determine eligibility for ACA premium tax credits for qualified individuals. These information reports will indicate if an employer offers coverage and, if so, whether it is affordable and adequate. In addition, the information reports will indicate whether an individual is covered by minimum essential coverage in order to avoid potential individual shared-responsibility payments. The same reports provided to the IRS must also be provided to each worker or covered individual, which will be used to document proof of coverage when they file their taxes in future years.

Table 3-1 summarizes which entity is responsible for each IRC section and the reporting requirements to the IRS and to workers. These details of the elements that are to be provided in these information reports are discussed as follows. The 1095-C and 1095-B Forms are at the employee level (similar to W-2s) and provide detailed information about the coverage provided to each employee. The 1094-C and 1094-B are transmittal forms that provide aggregate information about the number of 1095-C Forms submitted.

Table 3-1 IRS Reporting Requirements

Reporting Entity	IRC Section	ACA Provision	Information Forms Submitted to	
			IRS	**Workers or Insured**
Fully-Insured Plans				
Employers with 50 or more FTEs	6056	Employer shared-responsibility provision and premium tax credits	Form 1095-C And Transmittal Form 1094-C	Form 1095-C
All Insurers	6055	Individual shared-responsibility provision	Form 1095-B and Transmittal Form 1094-B	Form 1095-B
Self-Insured Plans				
Employers with 50 or more FTEs	Both 6056 and 6055	Both employer and individual shared-responsibility provisions	Form 1095- C and Transmittal Form 1094- C	Form 1095- C
Employers with less than 50 FTEs	6055	Individual shared-responsibility provision	Form 1095-B and Transmittal Form 1094-B	Form 1095-B

Source: Reprinted with permission from *Health Reform: What Small Businesses Need to Know Now!*, by Janemarie Mulvey, PhD.

Due Dates for Information Returns

Information statements from applicable large employers (ALEs) with 50 or more FTEs (Form 1095-C) and insurers (Form 1095-B) must be provided to workers and insured individuals on or before January 31 of the year immediately following the calendar year to which the information relates. However, for reporting in 2017 (for offers of coverage and coverage provided in 2016), employers were granted a 30-day extension from the general date. As a result, in 2017, 1095-C and 1095-B Forms are due to full-time workers and insured individuals on or before March 2, 2017.[1] Transmittal information reports (1094-C and 1094-B) and 1095-C and 1095-B Forms in paper format are due to the IRS on or before February 28 (March 31 if filed electronically) of the year immediately following the calendar year for which the coverage information is reported. Electronic returns are required if the reporting entity is required to file 250 or more information returns during the calendar year.

---

[1] See IRS Notice 2016-70.

KNOWLEDGE CHECK

1. Which form is NOT required by to be provided to workers in 2016 by self-insured employers with fewer than 50 FTEs?

    a. W-2.
    b. 1095-C.
    c. 1094-B.
    d. 1095-B.

Penalties for Noncompliance

Applicable employers and insurers are subject to penalties of up to $260 per return (not to exceed $3.19 million) for failure to comply with these reporting requirements.[2] These penalties were increased under the Trade Preferences Extension Act of 2105 from $100 per full-time employee with a maximum of $1.5 million which was initially stated in the ACA statute. There is, however, short-term relief for incomplete or incorrect returns filed or statements furnished to employees during the first year and second year (for coverage provided in calendar year 2015 and 2016). Specifically, the IRS will not impose penalties on entities with incorrect or incomplete returns that can show they made good faith efforts to comply with the information reporting requirements but whose returns are either incorrect or incomplete. Relief from penalties is provided for returns and statements filed and furnished in 2017 to report coverage in 2016, but only for incorrect or incomplete information. It is important to emphasize that the IRS will not provide relief from penalties for failure to file a return or statement by the March 31, 2017, deadline.

Information Required Under Employer IRS Reporting Requirements (1094-C and 1095-C Returns)

Under the ACA, the IRS added IRC Section 6056, which requires ALEs with 50 or more full-time employees (including FTEs) to file information returns (1094-C and 1095-C Forms) with the IRS and provide statements to their full-time employees about the health insurance coverage the employers offered. Included in these reports will be an indication of whether the insurance provided was affordable and provided minimum value.

Self-insured plans must also file this information as well as the insurer information discussed as follows. This information will be used to enforce and administer the ACA shared-responsibility provisions as well as help the IRS determine eligibility for premium tax credits.

These requirements apply to public and private employers as well as for-profit and not-for-profit (or tax-exempt) entities. The employer may be a single entity or may consist of a group of related entities, such as multi-employer plans or a parent or subsidiary or other affiliated entity (referred to as a controlled group).

---

[2] These penalties are consistent with IRC Sections 6721 and 6722 (penalties for failure to file correct information returns and to furnish correct payee statements) and are adjusted for inflation overtime.

KNOWLEDGE CHECK

2. What is the penalty for employers with 50 to 99 FTEs who do not file a 1094-C or 1095-C returns in 2016 for tax year 2015?

    a. $260 per return or up to $3.19 million.

    b. IRS will not levy a penalty for tax year 2015 for firms who do not file a return.

    c. $100 per full-time employee or up to $1.5 million.

    d. $260 per full-time employee or up to $3.19 million.

SPECIAL CONSIDERATION FOR RELATED ENTITIES

Multi-Employer Plans. A multi-employer plan is a plan maintained pursuant to one or more collective bargaining agreements and to which more than one employer is required to contribute. According to the IRS, employers that contribute to multi-employer plans may not have some of the information that is needed to report the preceding information. In order to comply with these requirements, the multi-employer plan administrator can prepare the returns pertaining to the full-time employees covered by the collective bargaining agreement. The contributing employer would prepare returns pertaining to its remaining full-time employees (those not eligible to participate in the multi-employer plan). The plan administrator would file a separate IRC Section 6056 return for each contributing employer, providing the name, address, and tax identification number (TIN) for the plan and the employer. The IRS requires the employer to file a single 6056 transmittal form (1094-C) reporting aggregate employer level for all full-time employees of the employer, including those covered by the collective bargaining agreement. In addition, employers that contribute to multi-employer plans must provide one 6056 employee statement (Form 1095-C) for each employee. The plan administrator may assist the employer in furnishing statements to its employees.

Controlled Groups. A controlled group is a combination of two or more corporations that are under common control within the meaning of IRC Section 1563(a). If the controlled group has more than 50 FTEs, then each member of the controlled group must file an information return with the IRS and furnish a statement to its full-time employees using its own employer identification number (EIN). For example, if an applicable large employer is comprised of a parent corporation and 10 wholly owned subsidiary corporations, there are 11 ALE members in this group. Each ALE member with full-time employees is the entity responsible for filing and furnishing statements with respect to its full-time employees. Conversely, subsidiary corporations that do not have full-time employees are not subject to the reporting requirement outlined in this chapter.

Government Entities. An employer who is a government entity and has been classified as an ALE may report under IRC Section 6056 or may designate another person or entity to file the return and furnish the statement to employees if that person is part of or related to the same governmental unit. Similar to the controlled group rule, a separate IRC Section 6056 return must be filed for each government ALE member. For example, the designated entity would provide the name, address, and EIN of both the designated entity and the ALE member for which it is reporting. Additionally, the IRS regulations require that there be a single Form 1094-C transmittal reporting aggregate employer level data for all full-time employees of the government entity.

INFORMATION TO BE REPORTED BY EMPLOYERS

To avoid potential ACA penalties for not providing adequate and affordable insurance,[3] employers must file a separate information return to the IRS using Form 1095-C for each full-time employee (similar to the W-2 Wage and Tax Statement). This information must also be provided to the full-time employee directly. There are two approaches allowed for reporting the required information to the IRS and individuals; the difference is in the level of detail under each approach:

- General method
- Alternative method(s)

Despite its name, the general method of reporting is the most comprehensive and requires employers to report more detailed information regarding the nature of their insurance coverage. For each employee, employers must file a return to the IRS and to each employee to verify monthly that the coverage they are providing meets the criteria of affordability (for example, employee contributions to premiums for self-only coverage does not exceed 9.66 percent of household income in 2016) and indicate what safe harbor provision they are using to determine affordability.[4]

Two alternative methods of reporting are provided by the IRS and were developed to minimize the cost and administrative tasks for employers and, in certain situations, may permit employers to provide less detailed information than under the general method for reporting. This section describes each method and identifies which employers are able to use the alternative simplified method versus the general method.

For the 2016 calendar year, the transition relief described as follows is applicable only if an ALE member offers coverage under a health plan with a non-calendar year plan.[5]

- **Coverage of Dependents of Full-time Workers.** Dependent coverage not required in months in 2016 that correspond to 2015 non-calendar plans because they are subject to transition relief in 2015.
- **95 Percent Rule.** In general, if an ALE does not offer minimum essential coverage to at least 95 percent of its full-time employees and their dependents, it may owe an employer shared-responsibility payment based on its total number of full-time employees. But non-calendar year plans overlapping between 2015 and 2016 are allowed to use the 70 percent coverage rate.
- **Penalty Formula.** If an ALE is subject to the employer shared-responsibility payment because it doesn't offer minimum essential coverage to its full-time employees and their dependents, the annual payment is generally $2,000 for each full-time employee—adjusted for inflation—after excluding the first 30 full-time employees from the calculation. For 2015 non-calendar year plans, if an ALE with 100 or more full-time employees (including FTEs) is subject to this employer shared-responsibility payment, the payment will be calculated by reducing the ALE's full-time employees by 80, rather than 30.

To certify that an employer falls in one or more of these transition relief categories, ALE employers must check Box C on Line 22 of the 1094-C Form.

---

[3] Adequate coverage (also called minimum value) has an actuarial value of 60 percent and a plan is affordable if the individual's contribution for self-only coverage for the lowest cost plan does not exceed 9.66 percent of their household income.

[4] Because employers do not generally know a worker's household income, IRS has provided three safe harbors employers can use to determine whether a plan is affordable. They are W-2 income, hourly rate, and poverty level.

[5] See https://www.irs.gov/Affordable-Care-Act/Employers/Understanding-2015-Transition-Relief-under-Employer-Shared-Responsibility-Provisions.

THE GENERAL METHOD OF REPORTING

Transmittal Form Elements

Under the general method of reporting, employers must provide a transmittal of aggregate information relating to the coverage they provide their employees on the following items on Form 1094-C:

- Employer's name, address, and EIN
- Name and telephone number of the employer's contact person
- Calendar year for which information is reported
- Certification of whether the employer offered its full-time employees (and their dependents) the opportunity to enroll in minimum essential coverage under an eligible employer-sponsored plan by calendar month
- Identify months during the calendar year for which plan coverage was available
- Each full-time employee's share of the lowest-cost monthly premium (self-only) for coverage providing minimum value offered to that full-time employee under an eligible employer-sponsored plan, by calendar month
- Number of full-time employees for each month during the calendar year (not required if employer qualifies for alternative reporting)
- Name, address, and TIN (the Social Security number) of each full-time employee (but not dependents) during the calendar year and the months, if any, during which the employee was covered under the plan (not required if employer qualifies for alternative reporting)

Detailed Elements on Reports Provided to Workers and IRS

In order for the IRS to determine if the employer complies with the employee shared-responsibility penalty provisions (for example, IRC Section 4980H), the following information will be reported through the use of *indicator codes* for some information on Form 1095-C. These indicator codes will include the following:

- Information as to whether the coverage offered to full-time employees and their dependents under an employer-sponsored plan provides minimum value and whether the employee had the opportunity to enroll his or her spouse in the coverage
- The total number of employees by calendar month
- Whether an employee's effective date of coverage was affected by a permissible waiting period
- Whether an employer had no employees or otherwise credited any hours of service during any particular month, by calendar month
- Whether the employer is part of a *controlled group* and, if applicable, the name and EIN of each employer member of the aggregated group constituting the applicable large employer
- If an appropriately designated person is reporting on behalf of an ALE member that is a governmental unit or any agency or instrumentality thereof for purposes of Form 1095-C, the name, address, and ID of the appropriately designated person must be provided
- If an ALE member is a contributing employer to a multiemployer plan, whether with respect to a full-time employee, the employer is not subject to an assessable payment under Section 4980H due to the employer's contributions to the multiemployer plan
- If a third party is reporting for an ALE member with respect to the ALE member's full-time employees, the name, address, and ID number of the third party must be included

There are two alternative methods of reporting under Section 6056 that were developed to minimize the cost and administrative tasks for employers. According to the IRS, the alternative reporting methods, in certain situations, may permit employers to provide less detailed information than under the general method for reporting.

The two alternative reporting options and their implications for the level of detail provided on Forms 1094-C and 1095-C are discussed in the following sections.

Option 1: Reporting Based on Certification of Qualifying Offers (1094-C Line 22 Box A)

To be eligible to use this simplified alternative method, the employer must certify that for all months during the year it made a *qualifying offer* to one or more full-time employees.

To be considered a *qualifying offer* the following criteria must be satisfied:

- The employer offered coverage that met minimum value.
- The employees' monthly cost for employee-only coverage does not exceed 9.69 percent of the federal poverty level in the 48 contiguous states (for example, the monthly premium an employee pays cannot exceed $95 in 2016).
- An offer of minimum essential coverage also was made to the employees' spouses and dependents.

To certify a qualifying offer, the employer checks Box A on Line 22 of Form 1094-C and enters code 1A on Line 14 of the 1095-C return for all 12 months for full-time employees that received a qualifying offer. The employer does not have to fill out the employee's share of premiums per month on Line 15 of Form 1095-C.

However, in lieu of providing a Form 1095-C to its employees, the employer has the option to send a letter to workers providing the employee's name and contact information and directing the employee to IRS Publication 974, "Premium Tax Credits." In addition, the employer must also include the following statements:

- Under the qualifying offer option, the letter must state that for all 12 months of the calendar year, the employee and the employee's spouse and dependents (if any) received a qualifying offer and therefore are not eligible for premium tax credits.
- Under this option, the employer still must provide a 1095-C return to the IRS and a 1095-C Form to new employees who did not receive affordable and minimum value coverage for the entire year.

Option 2: Report without Separate Identification of Full-Time Employees (1094-C Box D)

Option 2 is available only if certain conditions are met. Specifically, the employer must certify on its 1094-C Box D that it offered affordable coverage meeting minimum value to at least 98 percent of its employees. For this purpose, coverage is considered affordable to the worker if it meets any of the affordability safe harbor provisions using one of the three proxies for household income (for example, W-2 income, poverty level, hourly rate of pay, or federal poverty level).

In addition, the employer must certify that it offered minimum essential coverage to the dependents (but not spouses) of 98 percent of its workers. This alternative method of reporting allows reporting 1094-C without identifying or specifying the number of full-time employees (in Part III(b) of 1094-C). However, it does not exempt the employer from any penalties that might apply for failure to report with respect to any full-time employee if requested by the IRS.

Copies of the Form 1095-C can be found at https://www.irs.gov/pub/irs-pdf/f1095c.pdf.

Detailed Q and A for completing the forms can be found at https://www.irs.gov/Affordable-Care-Act/Employers/Questions-and-Answers-about-Information-Reporting-by-Employers-on-Form-1094-C-and-Form-1095-C.

Detailed Elements for Insurer IRS Reporting Requirements

ACA also requires certain entities to file 1094-B and 1095-B returns to the IRS certifying the provision of minimum essential coverage to policyholders, their dependents, and spouses. They also must furnish a 1095-B Form to each primary insured individual along with the contact information of the insured. This information will be used by the IRS to prove compliance with the individual shared-responsibility provisions in the ACA.

Entities That Must File an Information Return Reporting Minimum Essential Coverage

Any entity that provides minimum essential coverage to an individual must report to the IRS and furnish statements to individuals, including the following:

- Health insurance issuers, or carriers for insured coverage (except for exchange plans and supplemental coverage)
- The employer (for example, plan sponsor) of a self-insured group health coverage
- The executive department or agency of a governmental unit that provides coverage under a government-sponsored program

In addition, government entities such as Medicare and Medicaid must provide 1094-B and 1095-B information reports to the IRS on behalf of their beneficiaries covered by their program. Also, the individual exchanges must report to the IRS a 1095-A Form to individuals receiving coverage through the exchange.

The statements to individuals must be mailed first class to the last known permanent address of the primary insured (for example, responsible individual); or, if no permanent address is known, to the individual's temporary address. A health coverage provider also may furnish the statement electronically to the responsible individuals if they affirmatively consent to it.

Information That Must Be Reported

The information that an insurance provider must report to the IRS includes the following:

- The name, address, and EIN of the provider
- The primary insured individual's name, address, and TIN, which is typically his or her Social Security number, or date of birth if a TIN is not available
- The name and TIN, or date of birth if a TIN is not available, of each individual covered under the policy or program and the months for which the individual was enrolled in coverage and entitled to receive benefits
- For coverage provided by a health insurer through a group health plan, the name, address, and EIN of the employer sponsoring the plan and whether the coverage is a qualified health plan enrolled through the Small Business Health Options Program (SHOP) and (except for 2014 coverage reported in 2015) the SHOP's identifier.

Insurers may have difficulty getting the insured's TIN (or SSN) because, in today's world of cyber security threats, individuals may be reluctant to provide this information. A health coverage provider will not be subject to a penalty if it demonstrates that it properly solicited the TIN but was unable to obtain it. Under IRS guidance, the reporting entity must make an initial solicitation at the time the relationship with the payee is established. If the reporting entity does not receive the TIN, the first annual solicitation is generally required by December 31 of the year in which the payee enrolls in the plan (January 31 of the following year if the relationship begins in December). Generally, if the TIN is still not provided, a second solicitation is required by December 31 of the following year. If a TIN is still not provided, the reporting entity need not continue to solicit a TIN and can use date of birth.

Self-Insured Plan Information Reporting Requirements

Because self-insured plans are both employers and insurers, they must also report that they provide minimum essential coverage. Self-insured plans with 50 or more FTEs do not have to file a separate 1095-B Form. Rather they can report this information as part of their required 1095-C filings by filling out Part III on that form identifying the individuals covered under the policy.

Self-insured employers with less than 50 FTEs are not subject to the employer shared-responsibility provisions and therefore are not required to file 1094-C and 1095-C Forms with the IRS. However, because they are providing minimum essential coverage, self-insured employers with less than 50 FTEs do have to file 1094-B and 1095-B returns.

SPECIAL CONSIDERATION FOR RELATED ENTITIES WITH SELF-INSURED PLANS

Controlled Group. If the controlled group does not have 50 or more FTEs in the aggregate, and they are not reporting as an employer, they may report under IRC Section 6055 as separate entities or have one entity report for the controlled group.

Government Entity. Unless prohibited by other law, a government employer that maintains a self-insured group health plan may designate a related governmental unit, or an agency or instrumentality of a governmental unit, as the person to file the returns and furnish the statements for some or all individuals covered under that plan.

W-2 Reporting Requirements

Under the ACA, employers were required to report the total value of the health insurance coverage they provided to their employees on their employees' annual Form W-2. In box 12 DD of the W-2, the total value of health insurance coverage should include both the employer and the employee contributions and should use the same methodology used to calculate COBRA premiums. The amount reported will not include any amounts contributed to an Archer medical savings account or health savings account because these amounts are already required to be listed elsewhere on the W-2. In addition, the reported amount will not include any salary reduction contributions to a flexible spending arrangement made through a cafeteria plan. This provision does not change the tax treatment of an employer's contribution toward workers' premiums, which continue to be available on a pretax basis.

This provision was initially effective for tax year 2011, but the IRS delayed implementation until tax year 2012 for larger employers who file 250 or more W-2 Forms annually. Employers who file fewer than 250 W-2s annually have been provided transitional relief until further guidance is provided by the IRS. Further guidance must include at least six calendar months of advance notice of any change to the transition relief. As of the publication of this guide, no further guidance has been provided, but employers subject to transition relief can provide the required W-2 information on a voluntary basis.

OTHER REPORTING AND DISCLOSURE REQUIREMENTS

In addition to information reports submitted to the IRS, employers subject to the fair labor standards act (FLSA) are required to provide employees written notice concerning: (*a*) the existence of an exchange, including services and contact information; (*b*) the employee's potential eligibility for premium credits and cost-sharing subsidies if the employer plan's share of covered health care expenses is less than 60 percent; and (c) the employee's potential loss of any employer contribution if the employee purchases a plan through an exchange.

In general, the FLSA applies to employers that employ one or more employees who are engaged in, or produce goods for, interstate commerce. For most firms, a test of not less than $500,000 in annual dollar volume of business applies. The FLSA also specifically covers the following entities: hospitals; institutions primarily engaged in the care of the sick, the aged, mentally ill, or disabled who reside on the premises; schools for children who are mentally or physically disabled or gifted; preschools, elementary, and secondary schools, and institutions of higher education; and federal, state, and local government agencies.

The Department of Labor has provided sample notifications on their website for employers to use if they desired to do so. There are two notices—one if employers provide coverage and one if they do not. These model notices can be found at

- www.dol.gov/ebsa/pdf/FLSAwithplans.pdf or
- www.dol.gov/ebsa/pdf/FLSAwithoutplans.pdf.

The effective date for providing written notice to its existing employees about the Health Insurance Marketplace by October 1, 2013, and for new hires in 2014 within 14 days of being hired. However, because there has been no final regulation issued, there is no fine or penalty under the law for failing to provide the notice at this time.

KNOWLEDGE CHECK

3. A firm has fewer than 250 W-2 workers and is subject to the FLSA. Which are NOT required to provide to workers until further regulatory guidance is issued?

    a. Notice about the existence of an exchange in their state.
    b. The total value of health insurance coverage provided on W-2 Form.
    c. Eligibility for premium credits.
    d. Loss of employer premium contributions if purchased coverage in the exchange.

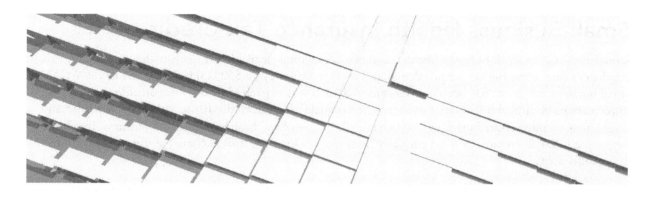

Chapter 4

SMALL BUSINESS TAX CREDIT, SHOP EXCHANGE, AND OTHER ACA TAX CHANGES IMPACTING INDIVIDUALS

LEARNING OBJECTIVES

After completing this chapter, you should be able to do the following:

- Identify which firms are eligible for small business tax credit given average wages and firm size.
- Identify which workers are included in the FTE calculation and which ones coverage is eligible for small business tax credit.
- Estimate amount of tax credit eligible for given firm characteristics and premiums.
- Identify effective dates of other ACA tax provisions.
- Determine if tax filer is subject to additional Medicare tax and estimate amount of tax.
- Identify ACA changes to tax-advantaged health accounts.

Small Business Health Insurance Tax Credit

Under the ACA, a small business health insurance tax credit is available for firms with less than 25 employees (including full-time equivalents) and average wages up to $52,000 in 2015.[1] While the ACA small business tax credit has been in effect since 2010, it was expanded in 2014 to coincide with the implementation of health insurance exchanges.[2] To qualify for the credit, firms within this firm size and wage category must contribute up to 50 percent of their workers' health insurance premiums. In addition, beginning in 2014, employers must enroll their employees in the SHOP exchange if it is available in their geographic area.

Small employers can claim the *full credit* amount (50 percent for for-profit and 35 percent for not for profit) if they meet the following two criteria:

- The employer has ten or fewer full-time equivalents (FTEs)
- The employer's average taxable wages are under $25,000 The credit is phased out as the number of FTEs increases from 10 to 25 and as average employee compensation increases from $25,000 to $50,000 (equivalent to $52,000 in 2016 after adjustments for inflation)

DETERMINING FIRM SIZE

To be eligible for the health insurance tax credits, firms must calculate their firm size based on a count of their full-time equivalent employees. FTEs include all *full-time employees plus part-time employees* aggregated up to FTEs. In calculating the FTE, there are three important determinants:

- Definition of an employee
- Definition of *full-time*
- Method used to calculate hours worked

Definition of Employees

The tax credit only applies to the health insurance premium contributions for a small business's employees. Generally, an employee is a common law employee,[3] a distinction that also includes those employees who meet one of the following:

- Terminate employment during the year for which the credit is being claimed,
- Covered under a collective bargaining agreement, or
- Do not choose to accept employer coverage offered (through the SHOP exchange).

---

[1] Eligible small employers are to use IRS Form 8941, "Credit for Small Employer Health Insurance Premiums," www.irs.gov/pub/irs-pdf/f8941.pdf or Form 990-T, "Exempt Organization Business Income Tax Return."

[2] For tax years 2010 to 2013, the maximum credit was 35 percent for for-profit firms and 25 percent for not-for-profit firms.

[3] As defined in IRC Section 45R-(a)(5). A discussion and example are available at www.irs.gov/Businesses/Small-Businesses-&-Self-Employed/Employee-Common-Law-Employee.

According to the IRS, a *leased employee* who is not a common law employee is considered an employee for tax credit purposes if he or she does all of the following:

- Provides services to the employer under an agreement between the employer and the leasing agency,
- Has performed services for the employer substantially full time for at least one year, and
- Performs services under an employer's primary direction or control.

Thus an employer cannot use hours, wages, or premiums paid with respect to a leased employee's initial year of service.

Not everyone who works at a firm is considered an employee and thus should be included in the FTE calculation. For example, for calculating the number of FTEs and their wages, the term "employees" excludes *seasonal workers* (working no more than 120 days during the year). However, premiums paid on behalf of seasonal workers are counted in determining the amount of the credit. Seasonal workers include retail workers employed exclusively during holiday seasons or during the summer. But if the firm provides health insurance to the seasonal worker and meets other requirements, it can claim a credit for its contributions to health insurance.

According to IRS regulatory guidance as shown in table 4-1, the IRS specifically states that the small business tax credit does not apply to health insurance provided to persons in the following categories:

- A 2-percent shareholder in an S-corporation
- A 5-percent owner of an eligible small business

In addition, the business will not receive a tax credit for the owner of a small business or his or her family members who may work for the business. The self-employed also cannot use the small business health insurance tax credit but can use individual premium tax credits available to anyone who meets the income thresholds regardless of work status.

Definition of Full-Time

In calculating the FTE, the definition of full-time and the determination of hours worked as well as the time period for measuring are different for the purposes of the tax credit as compared to other provisions within the ACA, such as potential employer penalties. For the small business health insurance tax credit, *full-time* is defined as 40 hours per week, or 2,080 hours a year.[4]

---

[4] This is different than the definition of *full-time* for purposes of the employer penalty, which is based on a 30 hour work week and is calculated based on a monthly average.

Table 4-1 Employees Included in FTE and Average Wages for Eligibility for Small Business Health Insurance Tax Credit

Type of Employee	Counted as FTE for Firm Size Calculation	Wages Included in the Average Amount	Employer Premium Contributions Eligible for Tax Credit
Owners			
Sole Owner of Business	No	No	No
S-Corp 2% or 5% Shareholder	No	No	No
Self-Employed	No	No	No
Family Members Employed by any of the Above	No	No	No
Employees			
Full-Time Workers (40 or more hours a week)	Yes	Yes	Yes
Seasonal Workers (<120 days)	No	No	Yes
Part-Time Workers	Yes	Yes	Yes
Leased Employees (Temps)	Yes, under certain circumstances	Yes, under certain circumstances	Yes, under certain circumstances

Source: Reprinted with permission from *Health Reform: What Small Businesses Need to Know Now!* by Janemarie Mulvey.

An employee's hours of service for a year include each hour for which an employee is paid or entitled to payment for the performance of duties during the employer's taxable year. It also includes each hour for which an employee is paid or entitled to be paid by the employer on account of a period of time during which no duties are performed due to vacation, holiday, illness, disability, jury duty, military duty, or leave of absence.

In calculating FTE, an employer can use different methods for different classifications of employees and any of the following three methods:

1. *Actual Hours Worked:* An employer may use the actual hours of service provided by employees (from records on which payment is made, such as timecards) including hours worked and hours for which payment is made or due.
2. *Days-Worked Equivalency:* An employer may use a days-worked equivalency whereby the employee is credited with 8 hours of service for each day for which the employee would be required to be credited with at least one hour of service.
3. *Weeks-Worked Equivalency:* An employer may use a weeks-worked equivalency whereby the employee is credited with 40 hours of service for each week for which the employee would be required to be credited with at least one hour of service.

The FTE Calculation

To determine FTE, a firm must add up each employee times the hours of service to get total hours of service over the entire year. Total hours of service are then divided by 2,080 to get an annual estimate of FTEs. If the result is not a whole number, it should be rounded to the next lowest whole number, with one exception. If the FTE is less than one then it should be rounded up to one FTE.[5]

KNOWLEDGE CHECK

1. Which of the following types of workers are included in *both*, the FTE calculation for purpose of determining eligibility for premium credit and the small business tax credit can be used toward their premiums?

    a. A family member who works for the company

    b. Seasonal workers working < 120 days

    c. Part-time workers

    d. None of the above

CALCULATION OF AVERAGE WAGES

The second criterion for eligibility for the small business health insurance tax credit is average wages below a certain threshold. All wages paid to employees (including overtime pay) are taken into account in computing an eligible small employer's average annual wages. Wages are defined as total wages on IRC Sect 3121(a) for purposes of FICA, including bonuses, but they do not incorporate the Social Security wage base limitation.

The average wage is determined by adding up total annual wages paid by the employer during the taxable year and dividing that number by the number of FTEs for the year (calculated above). If the result is not a multiple of $1,000, round down the result to the next lowest multiple of $1,000.

Employers of Multiple Entities

Employees of a *controlled group* (for example, multiple businesses with the same owner) are treated as those of a single employer for purposes of the tax credit, so total FTE and wages must be aggregated across all of the related entities. Controlled group rules are quite particular, and businesses should consult with their tax attorney to determine exactly what type of controlled group arrangement they have. IRS rules for determining whether an employer is a member of a controlled group or an affiliated service group are provided under IRC Sections 414(b), (c), (m), and (o).[6]

---

[5] See Worksheet 1 on IRS Form 8941 to calculate FTE: www.irs.gov/pub/irs-pdf/i8941.pdf.

[6] The IRS provides the following guidance on controlled groups: www.irs.gov/pub/irs-tege/epchd704.pdf.

AMOUNT OF THE CREDIT

To receive a credit, a small business must contribute at least 50 percent toward the employee's premium contribution. The share of the employer's premium contributions subject to the tax credit will vary depending on whether the firm is a for-profit (taxable) or not-for-profit (tax-exempt) firm.

For-Profit versus Not-For-Profit Firms

Beginning in 2014, the maximum credit is 50 percent of the for-profit employer's contribution toward premiums. This credit is "not refundable," in that it is limited by the for-profit employer's actual tax liability. In other words, if a for-profit company had a year in which it ended up paying no taxes (i.e., it had no taxable income after accounting for all its other deductions and credits), then the small business tax credit could not be used for that year; there would be no income tax for this credit to reduce. Similarly, if the firm had a tax liability less than the amount of the tax credit, the tax credit would be reduced to equal its tax liability. But as noted below, the tax credit can be carried forward and taken in future years.

For not-for-profit (tax-exempt) organizations, the credit will be up to 35 percent of the firm's premium contributions and will be paid in the form of a reduction in income and Medicare tax the employer is required to withhold from employees' wages plus the employer share of Medicare tax on employees' wages (with the credit thus limited by these amounts). For a tax-exempt eligible small employer, the amount of the credit cannot exceed the amount of the payroll taxes the employer is liable for during the calendar year in which the taxable year begins.

In addition, as part of its Internet portal, the Department of Health and Human Services provides an oponline calculator to determine the size of the small business health insurance tax credit: www.healthcare.gov/small-business-tax-credit-calculator/.

Health Insurance Contributions Eligible for the Credit

In order for small businesses to qualify for the credit in 2014 and following years, those with fewer than 25 employees must meet both of the following criteria:

- Contribute a uniform percentage of at least 50 percent toward their employees' health insurance premiums.
- Offer their employees insurance through the small business health options program (SHOP) exchange.[7]

The determination of the uniform whether the health insurer does composite or listing billing and is further complicated if an employer offers tiered coverage (for example, employee-only and family coverage).

Composite billing means a system of billing under which a health insurer charges a uniform premium for each employee or charges a single aggregate premium for the group of covered employees that the employer may then divide by the number of covered employees to determine the uniform premium. If an employer using composite billing pays the same percentage equal to at least 50 percent for each employee for employee-only coverage, the uniform percentage requirement is met. In the case of tiered coverage,

---

[7] The IRS has provided exceptions to enrolling in SHOP exchanges in regions where the SHOP is not yet available (see IRS Notice 2014-6).

the uniform percentage requirement is met if the employer contribution is at least 50 percent and the employer either

- pays the same amount for each employee enrolled in a particular tier of coverage, or
- pays an amount for each employee enrolled in a tier of coverage (other than employee-only coverage) that is the same for all employees and is no less than the amount that the employer would have contributed toward employee-only coverage for that employee.

List billing is defined as a billing system under which a health insurer lists a separate premium for each employee based on the age of the employee or other factors. In this case for employee-only coverage, the uniform percentage is satisfied if the employer either

- pays an amount equal to a uniform percentage (not less than 50 percent) of the premium charged for each employee, or
- determines an employer-computed composite rate, and if an employee contribution is required, each enrolled employee pays a uniform amount toward the employee-only premium that is no more than 50 percent of the employer-computed composite rate.

In the case of a plan that has list billing and tiered coverage, the employer satisfies the uniform percentage requirement if it either

- pays an amount for each employee covered under each tier of coverage equal to or exceeding the amount that employer would have contributed for that employee for employee-only coverage calculated either based upon the actual premium the insurer would have charged for that employee-only coverage or the employer-computed composite rate for employee-only coverage, or
- meets the requirements to employees offering one tier of coverage and substituting the computed composite rate for each tier of coverage.

The uniform percentage requirement is also applicable if the employer offers more than one plan through the SHOP exchange. In this case, the uniform percentage requirement can be determined on a plan-by-plan basis.

PARTIAL CREDIT: PHASE-OUT

The credit is phased out as the number of FTEs increases from 10 to 25 and as average employee compensation increases from $25,000 to $52,000. The credit phases out more rapidly with respect to firm size compared to increases in average wage. For example, a for-profit firm with fewer than 10 employees and average wages below $25,000 would qualify for a tax credit of 50 percent. If this small firm's employees received average wages of $45,000, the employer's tax credit would be 10 percent. If the small firm with average wages of less than $25,000 expanded to 24 workers, it would only receive a 2 percent tax credit.

Table 4-3 (see later in this section) shows the amount of the tax credit as a percentage (maximum of 35 percent) of the employer contribution toward workers' health insurance for not-for-profit businesses beginning in 2014.

Table 4-4 (see later in this section) shows the amount of the tax credit as a percentage (maximum of 50 percent) of the employer contribution toward workers' health insurance for for-profit businesses beginning in 2014. As shown in table 4-2, the value of the tax credit phases out significantly for employers with average wages equal to $45,000.

Table 4-2 Numerical Illustration of How Credit Works for For-Profit Firm With Fewer Than 10 Employees (2015)

Firm Characteristics	Average Premium Cost of Single Coverage	Employer Contribution	Tax Credit Available (Share of Contribution)	Employer's After-Tax Cost of Health Insurance (Share of Total Premium)
Average wages <$25,000	$5,400	$2,700	$1,350 (50%)	$1,350 (25%)
Average wages = $45,000	$5,400	$2,700	$270 (10%)	$2,430 (45%)

Source: Reprinted with permission from *Health Reform: What Small Businesses Need to Know Now!* by Janemarie Mulvey

LIMITATIONS TO THE SMALL BUSINESS HEALTH INSURANCE TAX CREDIT

Even if an employer meets the wage and firm size requirement discussed above, there are a number of limitations on the amount and use of the credit.

Time Period of the Credit. The small business tax credit is only available to an employer for two consecutive tax years, beginning with the first year that the employer offers coverage through a SHOP exchange.

Amount of Premium Contribution. The credit is not available based on the actual premium contributions of the employer. Rather, the employer contribution for purposes of determining the credit will be calculated as the *lesser of the*

* employer's actual premium contribution, or
* contribution the employer would have made if each of those same employees had enrolled in a Qualified Health Plan with a premium equal to the average for the small group market in the rating area in which the employee enrolls for coverage (see www.irs.gov/pub/irs-pdf/i8941.pdf for detailed premiums by locality).[8]

Coordination With Health Insurance Tax Deduction. Small firms that take a tax credit for health insurance coverage cannot also take a deduction for premiums paid under IRC Section 162.

---

[8] This average is determined by the secretary of HHS.

KNOWLEDGE CHECK

2. Which of the following statements is correct?

    a. The small business tax credit reimburses up to 50 percent of a non-profit employer's contributions to health insurance coverage if the employer also contributes at least 50 percent towards the plan premium.

    b. The credit is phased out as the number of FTEs increases from 10 to 25 and as average employee compensation increases from $25,000 up to $52,000.

    c. Employers can purchase coverage outside of the exchange and still receive the small business tax credit.

    d. The small business tax credit is only available to an employer for three consecutive years.

The Small Business Health Options Program (Shop) Exchange

Surveys of small businesses show that cost is the number one driver of whether or not they will offer health insurance coverage.[9] Compared to their larger competitors, smaller firms generally experience higher health insurance costs because of a number of factors. For one, they tend to have smaller risk pools in that the health costs of any single employee can drive up the overall premiums to the firm. For example, a small firm where one of its employees undergoes surgery or another expensive procedure could face substantially higher costs for its other workers enrolled in the same plan. Secondly, while the costs of administering the plan are largely fixed, for smaller firms, these fixed costs are spread across fewer enrollees, which raises their per-enrollee administrative costs.[10]

To help reduce the costs of insurance to smaller firms, the patient protection and affordable care act (ACA) enacted the small business health options program (SHOP) exchange to allow states to set up a marketplace for small businesses to purchase insurance with lower administrative costs and at more affordable rates. The individual state SHOP marketplaces are generally part of the individual marketplace (or exchange) in each state. States have the option to either: (1) set up their own state-based exchange, (2) rely on the federal government exchange, or (3) develop a partnership with the federal government.

To provide an added incentive for enrollment in the SHOP, small firms with less than 25 employees (including full-time equivalents) who want to take advantage of the small business tax credit must enroll their employees in the SHOP exchange beginning in 2014.

The SHOP exchanges have similar functions to the individual exchanges, including: collecting and verifying information from employers and employees, determining eligibility, and facilitating enrollment.

This section discusses the SHOP exchanges, including the following:

- Eligibility for SHOP
- Health plans offered in the SHOP
- Timeline for enrollment
- Role of brokers and agents
- Links to SHOP exchanges by state

ELIGIBILITY FOR SHOP

In order for a firm to be eligible for a SHOP exchange, it must meet the following criteria:

- Have a principal business address with the state where the firm is buying coverage, or have an eligible employee with a primary worksite within the state where coverage is being bought
- Have at least one common law employee[11] on payroll

---

[9] National Small Business Association, *2014 Small Business Health Care Survey*, February 2014.

[10] Linda J. Blumberg and L. M. Nichols, "Why Are So Many Americans Uninsured?" in *Health Policy and the Uninsured*, edited by Katherine G. McLaughlin (Washington, DC, Urban Institute Press, 2004).

[11] For the definition of a common law employee, visit IRS website: www.irs.gov/Businesses/Small-Businesses-&-Self-Employed/Employee-Common-Law-Employee.

- Be considered a small group under state definition (see determination of firm size below)
- Offer coverage to all full-time employees

Determining Firm Size

For employers to be qualified to use the SHOP exchange, they must be considered *small* group employers. Prior to 2016, the definition of a small group is determined by each individual state, with states having the option to define "small employers" as either having 100 or fewer employees or 50 or fewer employees. In 2016 and beyond, small employers will be defined as those with 100 or fewer employees.

Similar to the small business tax credit and the employer-shared responsibility payments, the determination of firm size is based on number of full-time workers and a calculation of full-time equivalents. However, the employees counted in FTE and those able to obtain coverage may be different than the other two provisions. This is because the definition of full-time employee, which is the basis of the FTE calculation, could vary for states that operate a state-based exchange. The definition of full-time as 30 hours a week (which is consistent with the employer penalty) is only required in the federally-facilitated SHOPs. State-based SHOP exchanges can use their own definition of full time until 2016, and it can be different than 30 or even 40 hours a week (which is the definition for the small business tax credit).

Definition of Employee

The definition of an employee is the same as described above for the ACA small business tax credit with respect to common law employees. So under this definition, the FTE calculation does not include seasonal employees working less than 120 days a year, or the business owners (2 percent shareholder in an S-corporation or 5 percent owner of an eligible small business), or the employed family of the owner.

However, once a business is determined to be eligible for coverage in the SHOP marketplace, business owners and their respective spouses may sign up for SHOP coverage.

TIMELINE FOR ENROLLMENT

For the 2016 benefit year, open enrollment rules in the SHOPs are determined by the states and are flexible. Generally, employers can begin shopping for coverage up to 3 months prior to the desired coverage effective date. Once the employer has selected the plans and contributions to make available to employees, the employer must select an open enrollment period during which employees can review their plan options.

SHOP EXCHANGES BY STATE

The individual state SHOP marketplaces are generally part of the individual marketplace (or exchange) in each state. States have the option to either (1) set up their own state-based exchange, (2) rely on the federal government exchange, or (3) develop a partnership with the federal government.

Among the state exchanges, 27 are federally-facilitated, meaning they are run through the federal government. Another 17 states have state-based marketplaces, with each state operating their own SHOP exchange.

The remaining seven states have what is called a partnership exchange. A partnership exchange is a *hybrid model* in which a state operates certain functions of a federally-facilitated exchange. A partnership exchange enables states to assume primary responsibility for carrying out certain activities related to plan management, consumer assistance, and outreach.

Table 4-3 Small Business Tax Credit as a Percentage (Maximum of 35 Percent) of Employer Contribution to Premiums, Not-for-Profit Firms in 2015

Firm Size (In FTEs)	Average Wage					
	Up to $25,000	$30,000	$35,000	$40,000	$45,000	$50,000
Up to 10	35.0%	28.0%	21.0%	14.0%	7.0%	0.0%
11	33.0%	26.0%	19.0%	12.0%	5.0%	0.0%
12	30.0%	23.0%	16.0%	9.0%	2.0%	0.0%
13	28.0%	21.0%	14.0%	7.0%	0.0%	0.0%
14	26.0%	19.0%	12.0%	5.0%	0.0%	0.0%
15	23.0%	16.0%	9.0%	2.0%	0.0%	0.0%
16	21.0%	14.0%	7.0%	0.0%	0.0%	0.0%
17	19.0%	12.0%	5.0%	0.0%	0.0%	0.0%
18	16.0%	9.0%	2.0%	0.0%	0.0%	0.0%
19	14.0%	7.0%	0.0%	0.0%	0.0%	0.0%
20	12.0%	5.0%	0.0%	0.0%	0.0%	0.0%
21	9.0%	2.0%	0.0%	0.0%	0.0%	0.0%
22	7.0%	0.0%	0.0%	0.0%	0.0%	0.0%
23	5.0%	0.0%	0.0%	0.0%	0.0%	0.0%
24	2.0%	0.0%	0.0%	0.0%	0.0%	0.0%
25	0.0%	0.0%	0.0%	0.0%	0.0%	0.0%

Source: Reprinted with permission from *Health Reform: What Small Businesses Need to Know Now!* by Janemarie Mulvey

Table 4-4 Small Business Tax Credit as a Percentage (Maximum of 50 Percent) of Employer Contribution to Premiums, For-Profit Firms in 2015 and Beyond

Firm Size (in FTEs)	Average Wage					
	Up to $25,000	$30,000	$35,000	$40,000	$45,000	$50,000
Up to 10	50.0%	40.0%	30.0%	20.0%	10.0%	0.0%
11	47.0%	37.0%	27.0%	17.0%	7.0%	0.0%
12	43.0%	33.0%	23.0%	13.0%	3.0%	0.0%
13	40.0%	30.0%	20.0%	10.0%	0.0%	0.0%
14	37.0%	27.0%	17.0%	7.0%	0.0%	0.0%
15	33.0%	23.0%	13.0%	3.0%	0.0%	0.0%
16	30.0%	20.0%	10.0%	0.0%	0.0%	0.0%
17	27.0%	17.0%	7.0%	0.0%	0.0%	0.0%
18	23.0%	13.0%	3.0%	0.0%	0.0%	0.0%
19	20.0%	10.0%	0.0%	0.0%	0.0%	0.0%
20	17.0%	7.0%	0.0%	0.0%	0.0%	0.0%
21	13.0%	3.0%	0.0%	0.0%	0.0%	0.0%
22	10.0%	0.0%	0.0%	0.0%	0.0%	0.0%
23	7.0%	0.0%	0.0%	0.0%	0.0%	0.0%
24	3.0%	0.0%	0.0%	0.0%	0.0%	0.0%
25	0.0%	0.0%	0.0%	0.0%	0.0%	0.0%

Source: Reprinted with permission from *Health Reform: What Small Businesses Need to Know Now!* by Janemarie Mulvey

Other ACA Tax Changes Impacting Individuals

The ACA introduced some additional taxes on high-income tax filers to finance the expansion of health insurance coverage to the uninsured. These additional taxes include an add-on to the Medicare payroll tax and additional taxes on net investment income. Some additional revenues were also raised limitations on tax advantaged accounts relating to health care (such as flexible spending and health savings accounts) and on itemized deductions used to pay for health care expenses.

Finally, beginning in 2020, there will be a 40 percent excise tax on health insurers whose plans they provide exceed certain thresholds.[12]

ADDITIONAL MEDICARE PAYROLL TAX

Under current law, employers and employees each pay a payroll tax of 1.45 percent to finance Medicare Hospital Insurance (Part A). ACA enacted additional Medicare Part A taxes on high-income taxpayers. Specifically, ACA imposes an additional payroll tax of 0.9 percent on high-income workers with wages over $200,000 for single filers and $250,000 for joint filers effective for taxable years after December 31, 2012. Married taxpayers filing separately are subject to a $125,000 threshold. The additional payroll taxes applies to wages above these thresholds. These income thresholds are *not indexed* for inflation in the future. Thus, the hospital insurance portion of the payroll taxes increases from 1.45 percent to 2.35 percent for wage income over the threshold amounts. The revenues from this provision are transferred directly into the Medicare Hospital Insurance Trust Fund (Part A).

Definition of Income Subject to Additional Medicare Tax

An individual will owe Additional Medicare Tax on wages, compensation and self-employment income (and that of the individual's spouse if married filing jointly) that exceed the applicable threshold for the individual's filing status. Medicare wages and self-employment income are combined to determine if income exceeds the threshold. A self-employment loss is not considered for purposes of this tax. Railroad Retirement Tax Act (RRTA) compensation is separately compared to the threshold.

The value of taxable wages not paid in cash, such as noncash fringe benefits, are subject to Additional Medicare Tax, if, in combination with other wages, they exceed the individual's applicable threshold. Noncash wages are subject to Additional Medicare Tax withholding, if, in combination with other wages paid by the employer, they exceed the upper income withholding thresholds. In addition, tips are subject to Additional Medicare Tax, if, in combination with other wages, they exceed the individual's applicable threshold.

An employer must withhold additional Medicare tax from wages it pays to an individual in excess of $200,000 in a calendar year, without regard to the individual's filing status or wages paid by another employer. An individual may owe more than the amount withheld by the employer, depending on the individual's filing status, wages, compensation, and self-employment income. In that case, the individual should make estimated tax payments and/or request additional income tax withholding using Form W-4, Employee's Withholding Allowance Certificate.

---

[12] The effective date on the excise tax on high-cost plans was extended by Congress as part of the 2016 budget deal (P.L. 114-113: Consolidated Appropriations Act 2016).

TREATMENT OF SELF-EMPLOYMENT TAX AND FICA WHEN WAGES EXCEED THRESHOLDS

Individuals with wages subject to FICA tax and self-employment income subject to SECA tax calculate their liabilities for Additional Medicare Tax in three steps:

Step 1. Calculate Additional Medicare Tax on any wages in excess of the applicable threshold for the filing status, without regard to whether any tax was withheld.

Step 2. Reduce the applicable threshold for the filing status by the total amount of Medicare wages received, but not below zero.

Step 3. Calculate Additional Medicare Tax on any self-employment income in excess of the reduced threshold.

Example. D and E are married and file jointly. D has $150,000 in wages and E has $175,000 in self-employment income. D's wages are not in excess of the $250,000 threshold for joint filers, so D and E are not liable for Additional Medicare Tax on D's wages. Before calculating the Additional Medicare Tax on E's self-employment income, the $250,000 threshold for joint filers is reduced by D's $150,000 in wages resulting in a reduced self-employment income threshold of $100,000. D and E are liable to pay Additional Medicare Tax on $75,000 of self-employment income ($175,000 in self-employment income minus the reduced threshold of $100,000).

KNOWLEDGE CHECK

3. Which of the following tax units is *not subject* to the additional Medicare payroll tax of 0.9 percent in 2016?

    a. Wages equal to $251,000 for joint filers.
    b. Wages equal to $126,000 for a single filer.
    c. Wages equal to $126,000 for married filing separately taxpayers.
    d. Wages equal to $201,000 for a single filer.

NET INVESTMENT INCOME TAX

The ACA also imposes an additional tax on net investment income for tax filers with income over specific thresholds. Net investment income is defined to be interest, dividends, non-qualified annuities, royalties, rents, and taxable capital gains. It excludes distributions from a qualified annuity from a pension plan.[13] The net investment income tax only applies if MAGI is over $250,000 for joint fillers, $125,000 for married filing separately, and $200,000 for all other returns.

---

[13] As defined in IRC Sec. 401(a), 403(a), 403(b), 408, 408A, or 457(b).

Specifically, effective for taxable years after December 31, 2012 tax filers will pay a tax equal to 3.8 percent of the *lesser of*

- net investment income for such taxable year, or
- the excess of MAGI over $250,000 for joint filers ($125,000 for married filing separately and $200,000 for all other returns).

It is important to note that if an individual has net investment income but does not have MAGI over these thresholds they will not pay a net investment income tax. Furthermore, sales from a principal residence are still subject to a partial exclusion from the tax under current law.[14] The net investment income tax will only apply to capital gains from the sale of a primary residence included in taxable income (i.e. capital gains over the exclusion amount) on if taxpayers MAGI exceeded the above thresholds.

Specifically, net investment income tax applies to the following:

- Interest
- Dividends
- Capital Gains
- Rental Income
- Royalty Income
- Non-qualified annuities
- Businesses
  - "Day traders"
  - Passive activities

It is important to note that net investment income does not apply to qualified annuities offered through an employer-sponsored defined benefit pension plan. However, pension income is included in MAGI.

While the net investment income tax is applicable to income from estates and trusts, the active income from self-employed and S-corporations would not be subject to the tax. For these pass-through entities, the tax will apply only to passive income and income related to commodity trading. There is also a special provision for the application of the tax to S-corporations who sell their business.

INCLUSION OF ESTATES AND TRUSTS AS NET INVESTMENT INCOME

Estates and trusts are subject to the Net Investment Income Tax if they have undistributed Net Investment Income and also have adjusted gross income over the dollar amount at which the highest tax bracket for an estate or trust begins for such taxable year under section 1(e) (for tax year 2015, this threshold amount is $12,300).

The following trusts are not subject to the Net Investment Income Tax:

- Trusts that are exempt from income taxes imposed by Subtitle A of the Internal Revenue Code (for example, charitable trusts and qualified retirement plan trusts exempt from tax under section 501, and Charitable Remainder Trusts exempt from tax under section 664).

---

[14] Under IRC Sect. 121, up to $250,000 single and $500,000 married in capital gains from sale of a principal residence are excluded from capital gains tax.

- A trust or decedent's estate in which all of the unexpired interests are devoted to one or more of the purposes described in section 170(c)(2)(B).
- Trusts that are classified as "grantor trusts" under sections 671-679.
- Trusts that are not classified as "trusts" for federal income tax purposes (for example, Real Estate Investment Trusts and Common Trust Funds).
- Electing Alaska Native Settlement Trusts.
- Perpetual Care (Cemetery) Trusts.

KNOWLEDGE CHECK

4. Tom just sold his house that he lived in for over 20 years. He recently divorced but had capital gains of $200,000 from the sale of the house. His total MAGI is $310,000. He also has some pension income of $80,000 and income from interest and dividends of $50,000. How much tax will he owe on net investment income in 2016?

    a. $4,180.
    b. $4,940.
    c. $1,900.
    d. $9,500.

CHANGES TO TAX-ADVANTAGED ACCOUNTS AND ITEMIZED DEDUCTIONS USED TO PAY FOR HEALTH CARE EXPENSES

A number of tax-advantaged accounts and tax deductions for health care spending and coverage were impacted by the ACA. These changes fall into two key areas:

- Tax-advantaged accounts for health care expenses
- Itemized deductions for medical expenses

Tax Advantaged Accounts for Health Care Expenses

Under current law, flexible spending accounts (FSAs), health savings accounts (HSAs), health reimbursement accounts (HRAs), and Medical Saving Accounts (MSAs) allow workers under varying circumstances to exclude a certain portion of qualified medical expenses from income taxes. Health FSAs are employer-established benefit plans that reimburse employees for specified health care expenses (for example, deductibles, co-payments, and non-covered expenses) as they are incurred on a pre-tax basis. According to the Bureau of Labor Statistics (BLS) survey, 39 percent of all workers in 2010 had access to a health care flexible spending account. Each employer may set their limits on FSA contributions, with most employers setting the maximum contribution limit to $5,000. Beginning in 2013, ACA will limit the amount of annual FSA contributions to $2,500 per account and index for general inflation in subsequent years. Given that the average annual contribution was $1,426 in 2009, this provision will not likely affect the average contributor to FSAs. However, the maximum limitation will impact those who have high out-of-pocket expenses.

HSAs are also tax-advantaged accounts that allow individuals to fund unreimbursed medical expenses (deductibles, copayments, and services not covered by insurance) on a pre-tax basis. Eligible individuals can establish and fund accounts when they have a qualifying high deductible health plan and no other health plan (with some exceptions). Unlike FSAs, HSAs may be rolled over and the funds accumulated over time. Distributions from an HSA that are used for qualified medical expenses are not included in taxable income. Distributions that are not used for qualified medical expenses are taxable as ordinary income and, under current law, an additional 10 percent penalty tax is imposed for those under the age of 65. ACA will raised this penalty on nonqualified distributions from 10 percent to 20 percent of the disbursed amount effective in 2011. Data are not available on the share of individuals taking HSA distributions for non-qualified expenses. However, account balances overall do increase significantly with the length of time the HSA is held. For example, in 2010, HSA balances for accounts held more than five years were $2,231 compared with $962 for those held for six months to one year. This would mean that, on average, the withdrawal penalty for non-qualified distributions for someone who held the account for more than five years would increase from $223 to $446 under ACA.

Effective in 2011, ACA modified the definition of qualified medical expenses. Under current law prior to ACA, qualified medical expenses for FSAs, HSAs, and HRAs could include over-the-counter medications. ACA restricts this practice and excludes over-the-counter medications (except those prescribed by a physician) as a qualified medical expense.

Modify Itemized Deduction for Medical Expenses

Prior to enactment of ACA, taxpayers who itemize their deductions may deduct unreimbursed medical expenses that exceed 7.5 percent of adjusted gross income (AGI). Medical expenses include health insurance premiums paid by the taxpayer, but also can include certain transportation and lodging expenses related to medical care as well as qualified long-term care costs, and long-term care premiums that do not exceed a certain amount. ACA increased the threshold to 10 percent of AGI for taxpayers who are under the age of 65 beginning in 2013, this effectively further limits the amount of medical expenses that can be deducted. Taxpayers over the age of 65 will be temporarily excluded from this provision and still be subject to the 7.5 percent limit from 2013 through 2016. Since the share of tax filers using the expense varies widely by age and income, this provision will adversely impact older households and those with lower incomes. While about 7 percent of all tax filers in 2008 (the most recent year for which published data are available) reported a deduction for medical expenses, 21 percent of tax filers aged 65 and older took the medical expense deduction and their deduction is 43 percent higher than the overall average for all tax filers. In addition, according to the JCT, taxpayers with AGI below $50,000 accounted for 41 percent of those taking this itemized deduction for medical expenses.[15]

---

[15]Joint Committee on Taxation, *Estimates of Federal Tax Expenditures for Fiscal Years 2010-2014*, December 15, 2010, JCS-3-10.

KNOWLEDGE CHECK

5. Which of the following statements is correct concerning ACA changes to tax-advantaged accounts and medical expense deductions?

   a. Effective 2013, the annual HSA contributions are limited to $2,500 which is adjusted for inflation

   b. Effective 2013, taxpayers over the age of 65 are allowed to deduct only medical expenses over 10 percent of AGI effective in 2013

   c. Effective 2013, annual FSA contributions are limited to $2,500 per account and this threshold is adjusted for inflation in future years.

   d. ACA changes now allow taxpayers to include over-the-counter medications as medical expenses when computing their itemized deductions.

GLOSSARY OF TERMS

Actuarial Value – A measure of the average value of benefits in a health insurance plan. It is calculated as the percentage of benefit costs a health insurance plan expects to pay for a *standard* population, using standard assumptions and taking into account cost-sharing provisions. The value only includes expected benefit costs paid by the plan and not premium costs paid by the enrollee.

Controlled Group – The Employee Retirement Income Security Act of 1974 (ERISA) added sections 414(b) and (c). These sections required that all employees of commonly controlled corporations, trades or businesses be treated as employees of a single corporation, trade or business. These Code provisions used the statutory definition of controlled groups found in IRC section 1563(a). ACA uses this definition of controlled group for eligibility under the employer-shared responsibility payments and IRS reporting requirements.

Dependent Coverage – Dependent health insurance coverage requires coverage of a child of an employee who has not attained age 26 as specified in IRC Section 152(f)(1). Dependent children under this definition is different than dependent children in other parts of the tax code and there is no requirement that the dependent currently resides with the parent nor does the parent have to claim them as a dependent on their taxes. This includes the entire calendar month in which the child turns 26. The definition of dependent in the ACA statute does not include the spouse of the employee.

Employer Shared Responsibility Payments (ESRP) – The Affordable Care Act requires certain employers with at least 50 full-time employees (or equivalents) to offer health insurance coverage to its full-time employees (and their dependents) that meets certain minimum standards set by the Affordable Care Act or to make a tax payment.

Individual Shared Responsibility Payments – Individuals who do not maintain minimum health insurance coverage and are not eligible for exemptions will be required to pay a penalty.

Modified Adjusted Gross Income (MAGI) – MAGI is adjusted gross income plus certain foreign income and tax-exempt interest and for the premium tax credit eligibility and affordability criteria under employer shared responsibility payments includes the nontaxable portion of Social Security income.

Federal Poverty Level (FPL) – The federal government's working definition of poverty that is used as the reference point to determine the number of people with income below poverty and the income standard for eligibility for public programs. The federal government uses two different definitions of poverty. The U.S. Census poverty threshold is used as the basis for official poverty population statistics, such as the percentage of people living in poverty. The poverty guidelines, released by the U.S. Department of Health and Human Services (HHS), are used to determine eligibility for public programs and subsidies including premium tax credits to subsidize health insurance coverage in the exchanges.

Individual Insurance Market – The market where individuals who do not have group (usually employer-based) coverage purchase private health insurance. This market is also referred to as the non-group market.

Medicaid – Enacted in 1965 under Title XIX of the Social Security Act, Medicaid is a federal entitlement program that provides health and long-term care coverage to certain categories of low-income Americans. States design their own Medicaid programs within broad federal guidelines. The ACA expanded Medicaid coverage to nontraditional households with income up to 138 percent of FPL (includes 5 percent set-aside).

Minimum Essential Coverage – The type of coverage an individual needs to have to meet the individual responsibility requirement under the Affordable Care Act. This includes individual market policies, job-based coverage, Medicare, Medicaid, CHIP, TRICARE, and certain other coverage.

Affordable Coverage – The definition of affordability varies between whether it is discussed in the employer shared responsibility payments or the individual shared responsibility payments. Under the employer provision, a plan is considered affordable to the employee if their share of the premiums for self-only coverage (for the lowest cost plan offered) does not exceed 9.5 percent of their household income (defined as MAGI).

Health Insurance Exchange (also called a marketplace) – State- or federally run and regulated insurance markets where a consumer can shop, compare, and buy health care coverage.

TAX GLOSSARY

401(k) Plan – A qualified retirement plan to which contributions from salary are made from pre-tax dollars.

Accelerated Depreciation – Computation of depreciation to provide greater deductions in earlier years of equipment and other business or investment property.

Accounting Method – Rules applied in determining when and how to report income and expenses on tax returns.

Accrual Method – Method of accounting that reports income when it is earned, disregarding when it may be received, and expense when incurred, disregarding when it is actually paid.

Acquisition Debt – Mortgage taken to buy, hold, or substantially improve main or second home that serves as security.

Active Participation – Rental real estate activity involving property management at a level that permits deduction of losses.

Adjusted Basis – Basis in property increased by some expenses (for example, by capital improvements) or decreased by some tax benefit (for example, by depreciation).

Adjusted Gross Income (AGI) – Gross income minus above-the-line deductions (such as deductions other than itemized deductions, the standard deduction, and personal and dependency exemptions).

Alimony – Payments for the support or maintenance of one's spouse pursuant to a judicial decree or written agreement related to divorce or separation.

Alternative Minimum Tax (AMT) – System comparing the tax results with and without the benefit of tax preference items for the purpose of preventing tax avoidance.

Amortization – Write-off of an intangible asset's cost over a number of years

Applicable Federal Rate (AFR) – An interest rate determined by reference to the average market yield on U.S. government obligations. Used in Sec. 7872 to determine the treatment of loans with below-market interest rates.

At-Risk Rules – Limits on tax losses to business activities in which an individual taxpayer has an economic stake.

Backup Withholding – Withholding for federal taxes on certain types of income (such as interest or dividend payments) by a payor that has not received required taxpayer identification number (TIN) information.

Bad Debt – Uncollectible debt deductible as an ordinary loss if associated with a business and otherwise deductible as short-term capital loss.

Basis – Amount determined by a taxpayer's investment in property for purposes of determining gain or loss on the sale of property or in computing depreciation.

Cafeteria Plan – Written plan allowing employees to choose among two or more benefits (consisting of cash and qualified benefits) and to pay for the benefits with pretax dollars. Must conform to Sec. 125 requirements.

Capital Asset – Investments (such as stocks, bonds, and mutual funds) and personal property (such as home).

Capital Gain/ Loss – Profit (net of losses) on the sale or exchange of a capital asset or Sec. 1231 property, subject to favorable tax rates, and loss on such sales or exchanges (net of gains) deductible against $3,000 of ordinary income.

Capitalization – Addition of cost or expense to the basis of property.

Carryovers (Carryforwards) and Carrybacks – Tax deductions and credits not fully used in one year are chargeable against prior or future tax years to reduce taxable income or taxes payable.

Conservation Reserve Program (CRP) – A voluntary program for soil, water, and wildlife conservation, wetland establishment and restoration and reforestation, administered by the U.S. Department of Agriculture.

Credit – Amount subtracted from income tax liability.

Deduction – Expense subtracted in computing adjusted gross income.

Defined Benefit Plan – Qualified retirement plan basing annual contributions on targeted benefit amounts.

Defined Contribution Plan – Qualified retirement plan with annual contributions based on a percentage of compensation.

Depletion – Deduction for the extent a natural resource is used.

Depreciation – Proportionate deduction based on the cost of business or investment property with a useful life (or recovery period) greater than one year.

Earned Income – Wages, bonuses, vacation pay, and other remuneration, including self-employment income, for services rendered.

Earned Income Credit – Refundable credit available to low-income individuals.

Employee Stock Ownership Plan (ESOP) – Defined contribution plan that is a stock bonus plan or a combined stock bonus and money purchase plan designed to invest primarily in qualifying employer securities.

Estimated Tax – Quarterly payments of income tax liability by individuals, corporations, trusts, and estates.

Exemption – A deduction against net income based on taxpayer status (such as single, head of household, married filing jointly or separately, trusts, and estates).

Fair Market Value – The price that would be agreed upon by a willing seller and willing buyer, established by markets for publicly-traded stocks, or determined by appraisal.

Fiscal Year – A 12-month taxable period ending on any date other than December 31.

Foreign Tax – Income tax paid to a foreign country and deductible or creditable, at the taxpayer's election, against U.S. income tax.

Gift – Transfer of money or property without expectation of anything in return, and excludable from income by the recipient. A gift may still be affected by the unified estate and gift transfer tax applicable to the gift's maker.

Goodwill – A business asset, intangible in nature, adding a value beyond the business's tangible assets.

Gross Income – Income from any and all sources, after any exclusions and before any deductions are taken into consideration.

Half-Year Convention – A depreciation rule assuming property other than real estate is placed in service in the middle of the tax year.

Head-of-Household – An unmarried individual who provides and maintains a household for a qualifying dependent and therefore is subject to distinct tax rates.

Health Savings Account (HSA) – A trust operated exclusively for purposes of paying qualified medical expenses of the account beneficiary and thus providing for deductible contributions, tax-deferred earnings, and exclusion of tax on any monies withdrawn for medical purposes.

Holding Period – The period of time a taxpayer holds onto property, therefore affecting tax treatment on its disposition.

Imputed Interest – Income deemed attributable to deferred-payment transfers, such as below-market loans, for which no interest or unrealistically low interest is charged.

Incentive Stock Option (ISO) – An option to purchase stock in connection with an individual's employment, which defers tax liability until all of the stock acquired by means of the option is sold or exchanged.

Income in Respect of a Decedent (IRD) – Income earned by a person, but not paid until after his or her death.

Independent Contractor – A self-employed individual whose work method or time is not controlled by an employer.

Indexing – Adjustments in deductions, credits, exemptions and exclusions, plan contributions, AGI limits, and so on, to reflect annual inflation figures.

Individual Retirement Account (IRA) – Tax-exempt trust created or organized in the U.S. for the exclusive benefit of an individual or the individual's beneficiaries.

Information Returns– Statements of income and other items recognizable for tax purposes provided to the IRS and the taxpayer. Form W-2 and forms in the 1099 series, as well as Schedules K-1, are the prominent examples.

Installment Method– Tax accounting method for reporting gain on a sale over the period of tax years during which payments are made, such as, over the payment period specified in an installment sale agreement.

Intangible Property– Items such as patents, copyrights, and goodwill.

Inventory – Goods held for sale to customers, including materials used in the production of those goods.

Involuntary Conversion – A forced disposition (for example, casualty, theft, condemnation) for which deferral of gain may be available.

Jeopardy – For tax purposes, a determination that payment of a tax deficiency may be assessed immediately as the most viable means of ensuring its payment.

Keogh Plan – A qualified retirement plan available to self-employed persons.

Key Employee – Officers, employees, and officers defined by the Internal Revenue Code for purposes of determining whether a plan is "top heavy."

Kiddie Tax – Application of parents' maximum tax rate to unearned income of their child under age 19. Full-time students under 24 are also subject to the kiddie tax.

Lien – A charge upon property after a tax assessment has been made and until tax liability is satisfied.

Like-Kind Exchange – Tax-free exchange of business or investment property for property that is similar or related in service or use.

Listed Property – Items subject to special restrictions on depreciation (for example, cars, computers, cell phones).

Lump-Sum Distribution – Distribution of an individual's entire interest in a qualified retirement plan within one tax year.

Marginal Tax Rate – The highest tax bracket applicable to an individual's income.

Material Participation – The measurement of an individual's involvement in business operations for purposes of the passive activity loss rules.

Mid-month Convention – Assumption, for purposes of computing depreciation, that all real property is placed in service in the middle of the month.

Mid-quarter Convention – Assumption, for purposes of computing depreciation, that all property other than real property is placed in service in the middle of the quarter, when the basis of property placed in service in the final quarter exceeds a statutory percentage of the basis of all property placed in service during the year.

Minimum Distribution – A retirement plan distribution, based on life expectancies, that an individual must take after age 70 ½ in order to avoid tax penalties.

Minimum Funding Requirements – Associated with defined benefit plans and certain other plans, such as money purchase plans, assuring the plan has enough assets to satisfy its current and anticipated liabilities.

Miscellaneous Itemized Deduction – Deductions for certain expenses (for example, unreimbursed employee expenses) limited to only the amount by which they exceed 2% of adjusted gross income.

Money Purchase Plan – Defined contribution plan in which the contributions by the employer are mandatory and established other than by reference to the employer's profits.

Net Operating Loss (NOL) – A business or casualty loss for which amounts exceeding the allowable deduction in the current tax year may be carried back two years to reduce previous tax liability and forward 20 years to cover any remaining unused loss deduction.

Nonresident Alien – An individual who is neither a citizen nor a resident of the United States. Nonresidents are taxed on U.S. source income.

Original Issue Discount (OID) – The excess of face value over issue price set by a purchase agreement.

Passive Activity Loss (PAL) – Losses allowable only to the extent of income derived each year (such as by means of carryover) from rental property or business activities in which the taxpayer does not materially participate.

Passive Foreign Investment Company (PFIC) – A foreign based corporation subject to strict tax rules which covers the treatment of investments in Sections 1291 through 1297.

Pass-Through Entities – Partnerships, LLCs, LLPs, S corporations, and trusts and estates whose income or loss is reported by the partner, member, shareholder, or beneficiary.

Personal Holding Company (PHC) – A corporation, usually closely-held, that exists to hold investments such as stocks, bonds, or personal service contracts and to time distributions of income in a manner that limits the owner(s) tax liability.

Qualified Subchapter S Trust (QSST) – A trust that qualifies specific requirements for eligibility as an S corporation shareholder.

Real Estate Investment Trust (REIT) – A form of investment in which a trust holds real estate or mortgages and distributes income, in whole or in part, to the beneficiaries (such as investors).

Real Estate Mortgage Investment Conduit (REMIC) – Treated as a partnership, investors purchase interests in this entity which holds a fixed pool of mortgages.

Realized Gain or Loss – The difference between property's basis and the amount received upon its sale or exchange.

Recapture – The amount of a prior deduction or credit recognized as income or affecting its characterization (capital gain vs. ordinary income) when the property giving rise to the deduction or credit is disposed of.

Recognized Gain or Loss – The amount of realized gain or loss that must be included in taxable income.

Regulated Investment Company (RIC) – A corporation serving as a mutual fund that acts as investment agents for shareholders and customarily dealing in government and corporate securities.

Reorganization – Restructuring of corporations under specific Internal Revenue Code rules so as to result in nonrecognition of gain.

Resident Alien – An individual who is a permanent resident, has substantial presence, or, under specific election rules is taxed as a U.S. citizen.

Roth IRA – Form of individual retirement account that produces, subject to holding period requirements, nontaxable earnings.

S Corporation – A corporation that, upon satisfying requirements concerning its ownership, may elect to act as a pass-through entity.

Saver's Credit – Term commonly used to describe Sec. 25B credit for qualified contributions to a retirement plan or via elective deferrals.

Sec. 1231 Property – Depreciable business property eligible for capital gains treatment.

Sec. 1244 Stock – Closely held stock whose sale may produce an ordinary, rather than capital, loss (subject to caps).

Split-Dollar Life Insurance – Arrangement between an employer and employee under which the life insurance policy benefits are contractually split, and the costs (premiums) are also split.

Statutory Employee – An insurance agent or other specified worker who is subject to social security taxes on wages but eligible to claim deductions available to the self-employed.

Stock Bonus Plan – A plan established and maintained to provide benefits similar to those of a profit-sharing plan, except the benefits must be distributable in stock of the employer company.

Tax Preference Items – Tax benefits deemed includable for purposes of the alternative minimum tax.

Tax Shelter – A tax-favored investment, typically in the form of a partnership or joint venture, that is subject to scrutiny as tax-avoidance device.

Tentative Tax – Income tax liability before taking into account certain credits, and AMT liability over the regular tax liability.

Transportation Expense – The cost of transportation from one point to another.

Travel Expense – Transportation, meals, and lodging costs incurred away from home and for trade or business purposes.

Unearned Income – Income from investments (such as interest, dividends, and capital gains).

Uniform Capitalization Rules (UNICAP) – Rules requiring capitalization of property used in a business or income-producing activity (such as items used in producing inventory) and to certain property acquired for resale.

Unrelated Business Income (UBIT) – Exempt organization income produced by activities beyond the organization's exempt purposes and therefore taxable.

Wash Sale – Sale of securities preceded or followed within 30 days by a purchase of substantially identical securities. Recognition of any loss on the sale is disallowed.

INDEX

HEALTH CARE REFORM ACT: CRITICAL TAX AND INSURANCE RAMIFICATIONS

BY JANEMARIE MULVEY, PH.D.

Solutions

The AICPA offers a free, daily, e-mailed newsletter covering the day's top business and financial articles as well as video content, research and analysis concerning CPAs and those who work with the accounting profession. Visit the CPA Letter Daily news box on the www.aicpa.org home page to sign up. You can opt out at any time, and only the AICPA can use your e-mail address or personal information.

Have a technical accounting or auditing question? So did 23,000 other professionals who contacted the AICPA's accounting and auditing Technical Hotline last year. The objectives of the hotline are to enhance members' knowledge and application of professional judgment by providing free, prompt, high-quality technical assistance by phone concerning issues related to: accounting principles and financial reporting; auditing, attestation, compilation and review standards. The team extends this technical assistance to representatives of governmental units. The hotline can be reached at 1-877-242-7212.

SOLUTIONS

CHAPTER 1

1.

   a.   Incorrect. This amount does not exclude the tax filing threshold from MAGI and is lesser, not greater than the fixed dollar amount.

   b.   Correct. The answer is the greater of a fixed dollar amount or percentage of MAGI-tax filing threshold. For 2016, the fixed dollar amount is the greatest at $695 per family member over age 18.

   c.   Incorrect. Although this is the correct calculation taking 2.5 percent of MAGI-tax filing threshold, it is less than the fixed dollar amount.

   d.   Incorrect. This is the 2015 fixed dollar amount.

2.

   a.   Incorrect. Although the individual shared responsibility payments are in effect, the IRS delayed reporting requirements until 2015. Individuals must self-report in 2014.

   b.   Incorrect. Although reporting requirements were required this year, due dates were extended past filing deadlines.

   c.   Incorrect. Due dates extended to March 2 which is past some filers filings. Just keep forms for documentation.

   d.   Correct. This is the first year they are required.

3.

   a.   Incorrect. Unlike other taxes and penalties for nonpayment, there is no additional fine for not paying individual shared responsibility payment, the payment will be deducted only from future refunds.

   b.   Incorrect. Unlike other taxes and penalties for nonpayment, there is no additional fine for not paying individual shared responsibility payment, the payment will be deducted only from future refunds.

   c.   Incorrect. Unlike other taxes and penalties for nonpayment, there is no additional fine for not paying individual shared responsibility payment, the payment will be deducted only from future refunds.

   d.   Correct. The law intentionally omitted additional financial or other penalties for fear the headlines would read: "Man goes to jail for not having health insurance coverage and failing to pay the penalty."

4.

    a.   Incorrect, non-taxable SSB are included in the affordability criteria for employer penalty.

    b.   Correct, non-taxable SSB are not included in the MAGI threshold for the net investment income tax threshold.

    c.   Incorrect, non-taxable SSB are included in the MAGI definition for determining eligibility for the premium Tax Credits.

    d.   Incorrect, non-taxable SSB are included in the MAGI definition for determining eligibility for the Medicaid Expansion.

5.

    a.   Incorrect. This would apply for a one-person family in Hawaii, and this example has a family size of three.

    b.   Correct. The income level for 400 percent of poverty for a family of three in Hawaii is $92,440, and this exceeds that level.

    c.   Incorrect. This would exceed the income level for family of three if the family resided in the 48 contiguous states.

    d.   Incorrect. This would apply for a two-person family in Hawaii, and this example has a family size of three.

6.

    a.   Correct. MAGI not taxable income is used to determine the premium tax credit.

    b.   Incorrect. Benchmark premium level that is eligible for claiming the premium tax credit is based on the second-lowest-cost "silver" plan in a taxpayer's geographic locality. This is used in the premium tax credit formula.

    c.   Incorrect. Family size will affect the amount of the premium tax credit.

    d.   Incorrect. The maximum premium contribution percentage is used in the premium tax credit formula.

CHAPTER 2

1.

    a.   Correct. Part-time workers hours are converted into FTEs by dividing by 120 per month.

    b.   Incorrect. Real estate agents and direct sellers are explicitly excluded as employees in the IRS regulations.

    c.   Incorrect. Independent contractors are not considered employees.

    d.   Incorrect. Two-percent S corporation stakeholders are not considered employees.

2.

    a.   Incorrect. Seasonal workers who work full-time for more than six months can trigger a penalty.

    b.   Incorrect. Full time workers can trigger a penalty.

    c.   Correct. Part-time workers even though they are included in the initial FTE calculation, they cannot trigger the penalty.

    d.   Incorrect. Temporary agency employees determined to be full-time, on average, for up to 12 months can trigger the penalty.

3.

  a. Incorrect. Under revisions to the law, employees with TRICARE or VA coverage are excluded from the FTE calculation.
  b. Correct. Although seasonal workers working fewer than 120 days are not included in FTE, those with 120 days or more are included.
  c. Incorrect. Real estate agents are not considered employees.
  d. Incorrect. Leased employees are not considered employees.

4.

  a. Incorrect. This is considered a proxy for monthly household income.
  b. Correct. Although this might provide household MAGI, it is not required for the company to determine affordability.
  c. Incorrect. This is considered a proxy for household income of the worker.
  d. Incorrect. This calculation is considered a proxy for the household income of the worker.

5.

  a. Incorrect. This is a random number.
  b. Correct. Answer = $2, 160 (150–30) – $259,200.
  c. Incorrect. This response excludes the 20 Medicare beneficiaries from count of full-time workers in choice *b*.
  d. Incorrect. This answer uses the 2014 penalty amount of $2,000 without adjusting for inflation.

6.

  a. Incorrect. This is a true statement: "The determination of ALE Status (that is, firm size) is based on the aggregate FTE count across all members of the controlled group."
  b. Incorrect. This is a true statement: "The determination of the penalty amount is based on the characteristics of each entity of the controlled group is levied separately for each."
  c. Correct. The determination of ALE status is based on the aggregate FTE count across all members of controlled group.
  d. Incorrect. This is a true statement: "The penalty is triggered by an individual entity of the controlled group. Therefore, it applies only to that member."

CHAPTER 3

1.

  a. Incorrect. Firms do have to submit a W-2.
  b. Correct. Self-insured firms with fewer than 50 FTEs do not have to submit a 1095-C to workers. Only larger firms with 50 or more have to submit 1095-C forms.
  c. Incorrect. This is a transmittal form that goes only to the IRS for self-insured firms with fewer than 50 FTEs.
  d. Incorrect. Because self-insured firms also have to submit insurance form 1095-B to workers to prove minimum essential coverage.

2.

    a.   Correct. The penalty to $260 per return or up to $3.19 million.

    b.   Incorrect. The IRS will levy a penalty for tax year 2016 for firms who do not file a return; however, they will not penalize incorrect filings.

    c.   Incorrect. Although the ACA initially set the penalty at $100 per employee or up to $1.5 million, it was changed under the Trade Preferences Extension Act of 2015.

    d.   Incorrect. The penalty is per return, not per employee.

3.

    a.   Incorrect. Notice of exchanges is required for all FLSA employers.

    b.   Correct. The IRS has provided temporary relief for employers with less than 250 W-2 workers until further guidance is issued.

    c.   Incorrect. Employers must notify workers whether or not they are eligible for premium tax credits under the ACA.

    d.   Incorrect. Employers must notify workers that if they purchase coverage in the exchange, they will not be eligible for employer premium contributions.

CHAPTER 4

1.

    a.   Incorrect. This worker would not be included in FTE, nor be eligible for employer contributions under the small business tax credit.

    b.   Incorrect. These workers would not be included in FTE calculation, but employer contributions for their coverage are eligible for the small business tax credit.

    c.   Correct. They are included in the FTE calculation, and employer premium contributions toward coverage are eligible for small business tax credit.

    d.   Incorrect. See preceding responses.

2.

    a.   Incorrect. Not-for-profit employers receive a tax credit of up to 35 percent of their contributions to health insurance coverage for their workers.

    b.   Correct. The credit is phased out as the number of FTEs increases from 10 to 25 and as average employee compensation increases from $25,000 up to $52,000.

    c.   Incorrect. Starting in 2014, employers must purchase coverage in the SHOP exchange to be eligible for the small business tax credit.

    d.   Incorrect. The small business tax credit is available only for two consecutive years.

3.

    a.   Incorrect. Wages greater than $250,000 for joint filers are subject to the additional Medicare tax.

    b.   Correct. Wages greater than $125,000, but less than $200,000, are not subject to the additional Medicare tax.

    c.   Incorrect. Wages greater than $125,000 for *married filing separately* taxpayers are subject to the additional Medicare tax.

    d.   Incorrect. Wages greater than $200,000 for a single filer are subject to the additional Medicare tax.

4.

a. Incorrect. This is the greater of 3.8 percent of $110,000 ($310,000 – $200,000, MAGI in excess of the threshold) compared to 3.8 percent if Net Investment Income(NII) = 3.8 percent of $50,000 which is the only source of income subject to NII). Note that the gain on the principal residence is excluded under current tax law.

b. Incorrect. Assumes that NII = $80,000 + $50,000; but pension income is not included.

c. Correct. This is 3.8 percent of $50,000 which is how much is considered net investment income counted and is lesser than (*a*).

d. Incorrect. It takes 3.8 percent of incorrect NII is $80,000 + $50,000 + $200,000 which include items that are not subject to NIIT.

5.

a. Incorrect. The annual HSAs contributions were not limited directly under the ACA.

b. Incorrect. The effective date for taxpayers over the age of 65 is 2017.

c. Correct. Effective 2013, annual FSA contributions are limited to $2,500 per account, and this threshold is adjusted for inflation in future years.

d. Incorrect. ACA restricts this practice and excludes over-the-counter medications (except those prescribed by a physician) as a qualified medical expense.

Learn More

AICPA CPE

Thank you for selecting AICPA as your continuing professional education provider. We have a diverse offering of CPE courses to help you expand your skillset and develop your competencies. Choose from hundreds of different titles spanning the major subject matter areas relevant to CPAs and CGMAs, including:

- Governmental & Not-for-Profit accounting, auditing, and updates
- Internal control and fraud
- Audits of Employee Benefit Plans and 401(k) plans
- Individual and corporate tax updates
- A vast array of courses in other areas of accounting & auditing, controllership, management, consulting, taxation, and more!

Get your CPE when and where you want

- Self-study training options that includes on-demand, webcasts, and text formats with superior quality and a broad portfolio of topics, including bundled products like –
  - ➢ CPExpress for immediate access to hundreds of one and two-credit hour online courses for just-in-time learning at a price that is right
  - ➢ Annual Webcast Pass offering live Q&A with experts and unlimited access to the scheduled lineup, all at an incredible discount.
- Staff training programs for audit, tax and preparation, compilation and review
- Certificate programs offering comprehensive curriculums developed by practicing experts to build fundamental core competencies in specialized topics
- National conferences presented by recognized experts
- Affordable AICPA courses on-site at your organization – visit **aicpalearning.org/on-site** for more information.
- Seminars sponsored by your state society and led by top instructors. For a complete list, visit **aicpalearning.org/publicseminar**.

Take control of your career development

The AICPA | CIMA Competency and Learning website at **https://competency.aicpa.org** brings together a variety of learning resources and a self-assessment tool, enabling tracking and reporting of progress toward learning goals.

Visit the AICPA store at cpa2biz.com/CPE to browse our CPE selections.

Just-in-time learning at your fingertips 24/7

Where can you get <u>unlimited online access</u> to 900+ credit hours (650+ CPE courses) for one low annual subscription fee?

CPExpress, the AICPA's comprehensive bundle of online continuing professional education courses for CPAs, offers you immediate access to hundreds of one and two-credit hour courses. You can choose from a full spectrum of subject areas and knowledge levels to select the specific topic you need when you need it for just-in-time learning.

Access hundreds of courses for one low annual subscription price!

How can CPExpress help you?

- ✓ Start and finish most CPE courses in as little as 1 to 2 hours with 24/7 access so you can fit CPE into a busy schedule
- ✓ Quickly brush up or get a brief overview on hundreds of topics when you need it
- ✓ Create and customize your personal online course catalog for quick access with hot topics at your fingertips
- ✓ Print CPE certificates on demand to document your training – never miss a CPE reporting deadline!
- ✓ Receive free Quarterly updates – Tax, Accounting & Auditing, SEC, Governmental and Not-For-Profit

Quantity Purchases for Firm or Corporate Accounts

If you have 10 or more employees who require training, the Firm Access option allows you to purchase multiple seats. Plus, you can designate an administrator who will be able to monitor the training progress of each staff member. To learn more about firm access and group pricing, visit aicpalearning.org/cpexpress or call 800.634.6780.

To subscribe, visit **cpa2biz.com/cpexpress**

Why AICPA?

Think of All the Great Reasons to Join the AICPA.

CAREER ADVOCACY SUPPORT
On behalf of the profession and public interest on the federal, state and local level.

PROFESSIONAL & PERSONAL DISCOUNTS
Save on travel, technology, office supplies, shipping and more.

ELEVATE YOUR CAREER
Five specialized credentials and designations (ABV®, CFF®, CITP®, PFS™ and CGMA®) enhance your value to clients and employers.

HELPING THE BEST AND THE BRIGHTEST
AICPA scholarships provide more than $350,000[1] to top accounting students.

GROW YOUR KNOWLEDGE
Discounted CPE on webcasts, self-study or on-demand courses & more than 60 specialized conferences & workshops.

PROFESSIONAL GUIDANCE YOU CAN COUNT ON
Technical hotlines & practice resources, including Ethics Hotline, Business & Industry Resource Center and the Financial Reporting Resource Center.

KEEPING YOU UP TO DATE
With news and publications from respected sources such as the *Journal of Accountancy*.

MAKING MEMBERS HAPPY
We maintain a 94%+ membership renewal rate.

FOUNDED ON INTEGRITY
Representing the profession for more than 125 years.

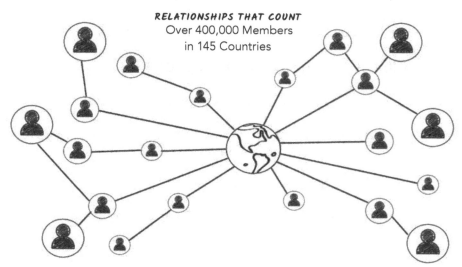

RELATIONSHIPS THAT COUNT
Over 400,000 Members in 145 Countries

TO JOIN, VISIT:
aicpa.org/join or call 888.777.7077.